TWELVE GREATEST MIRACLES
OF MY MINISTRY

TWELVE GREATEST MIRACLES OF MY MINISTRY

by
ORAL ROBERTS

FIRST PUBLISHED EDITION

FIRST PRINTING   100,000 FEBRUARY 1974

PRINTED IN THE UNITED STATES OF AMERICA

CONTENTS

Oral Roberts

CHAPTER ONE

THE GREATEST MIRACLE I EVER SAW IS THE ONE THAT HAPPENED TO ME

(My salvation, my healing from tuberculosis and stammering)

NOT LONG AGO, when I was a guest on the Merv Griffin Show he asked me a question that I've been asked many times. He said:

"ORAL, WHAT IS THE GREATEST MIRACLE OF YOUR ENTIRE MINISTRY?"

I said, "Merv . . . the greatest miracle I ever saw was *my own personal miracle* when God healed me of tuberculosis and loosed my stammering tongue. It was the greatest because it happened to me."

Merv's question that day inspired me to write this book. I wanted to share with you my personal miracle of healing, and some of the other great miracles that I have personally witnessed in this ministry of God's healing love. I want to do this because I believe everybody — at some time in his life — needs a miracle. I know I do — again and again. And I believe you do. I am praying that as you read this book it will help you to start expecting a miracle for your need . . . NOW! I pray that you will learn to live in expectancy of miracles.

I have learned that the very secret of life is in expecting miracles. In fact, I LIVE ON MIRACLES . . . I admit it. My very life and breath and speech is a miracle. For, you see, it was through a miracle of God that I received breath into my life . . .

I received a healing for my hemorrhaging lungs, and my stammering tongue . . .

I cannot but thank God for His miracle power.

Yet there was a time when I wouldn't have recognized a miracle if I had seen it coming down the road. I was too busy trying to make my own miracles, my own way. In fact, I had rebelled against my beautiful parents who loved God and believed in His power to perform miracles.

My father was a preacher and maybe one thing I rebelled against was that we were always poor. As the saying goes, we were "too poor to paint and too proud to whitewash." Even the poor people called us poor. The people who supported my father indicated by their actions, *God, if you will keep Rev. E. M. Roberts humble, we will keep him poor.* I tell you, that was hard to take when your stomach was empty, when you lived in a little two-room house, and you never had enough clothes to wear. But that really wasn't the thing that turned me off. It was something deeper inside me.

THERE WAS A REBEL INSIDE ME

I know what a lot of young people feel today as they turn off from their parents, the church, the establishment, or society. I felt a constant pain, like a knife in my ribs, that made me want to get away. To go, to run, to do my own thing. And I did get away. As far away as I could. I thought that would change things for me. The result was that I ran into more trouble.

One night when I was playing in a district basketball championship, I collapsed on the floor. My coach picked me up and the blood was running from my nostrils. He said,

"Son, I'm taking you home, back to your parents." I was too weak to resist.

He took me back to my mother and father in Ada, Oklahoma. I looked at their faces and I remembered what they had said, "Oral, you will never get so far but that we will be praying for you." If you have someone praying for you, it's worth more than diamonds and silver and gold.

You see, what happened . . .

I had turned God off.

The truth was that what they were and what they stood for was what I was against . . . and that was God and the implications of what He had planned for my life. I'd been born a stammerer — stammered all my life. The first day I went to school I tried to say my name and couldn't say it. Yet my name, *Oral*, means spoken word. They had misnamed me, apparently. Some reporters have thought *Oral* is a stage name but it is my real name. I was named Granville Oral, and they said, "We will call him Oral."

People laughed when I stuttered. It was funny to them, but it wasn't funny to me. Finally as I lay in the back seat of the coach's car, as he drove me back home, I realized I had RUN OUT OF LIFE. Just like a car runs out of gas. I ran out of life. My life stalled. When I was carried into my parents' house and laid on the bed, I looked up at my father and mother and I said, "I've gone the last mile of the way."

I lay there 163 days, hemorrhaging to death. Many times I cursed the day I was born.

I do not know where people get the idea that sickness is a blessing. I was the most miserable person in the world. I coughed and spit up blood and tossed on the bed day and night, not able to sleep more than a few hours at a time. I went as much as 48 hours without a wink of sleep. Food lost its taste. My weight dropped from 160 to 120 pounds. I was 6 feet 1½ inches tall, yet weighed only 120 pounds.

My friends no longer recognized me, and when they came to see me they said they couldn't stand to look at me.

One day Papa came over to my bed and looked down at me. His chin was quivering. Since the doctor had just been there and given me another examination, I knew Papa knew the verdict. I said, "Papa, what did the doctor say?" If I live to be a million years old I will never forget his answer.

"Oral, you have tuberculosis in both lungs."

It seemed that the whole world came crashing down upon my head. The sun slowly fell from the sky as I faced the end of my dreams. Black despair settled over my soul, and I began to cry. Turning my face to the wall, I let go. I cried so hard I screamed with pain. Papa came over and tried to pull me back across the bed, but I fought him off. I cried until there were no more tears left. My eyes became dry. My lips hard and set.

Every ambition I ever had was crushed in a moment. I felt lost and miserable.

Within a few days I felt death on my body. I didn't care. I wanted to die.

I lay there.

I felt forgotten by the world — my own ambitions crushed.

I had dreamed of becoming a lawyer and my great dream was to be governor of Oklahoma. But, now, I'm flat on my back and I can't get up. Life is over for me. Then . . .

GOD INVADED MY LIFE

One day my mother came to my room, sat down on my bed beside me, and began talking. She said God had spoken

to her about me before I was born, that I was His, and that
God's hand was upon my life.

I said, "Mamma, why do people say God put tuberculosis on me?"

She said, "Oral, God didn't put this disease on you."

I said, "Well, Mamma, if God didn't, who did?"

She said, "The devil did, Son. He is trying to destroy
your life."

I said, "Mamma, why is he trying to destroy me?"

She said, "The devil is trying to destroy everyone, and
especially when God calls someone to do His work, Son, the
devil always makes a special effort to destroy him. But if you
will give your heart to Jesus and have faith in the Lord, He
will raise you up from this bed and heal you."

That was the first time I ever had any idea that God
would heal anyone. But it was my sister Jewel who inspired
me to have hope in my heart that God would heal *me*. She
came to visit us about a week later. She came straight to my
bed and looked down at me. She said she had been praying
for me. Suddenly, with tears in her eyes, she said seven
words that changed my life. She said:

"Oral, God is going to heal you."

I said, "Is He, Jewel?"

She said, "Yes."

It was like all the lights of the world were turned on in
my soul. For the first time, I knew there was a God. In the
flash of a second I knew that He knew there was Oral
Roberts. I was a person. I was no longer a nonperson, lying
there dying. Somebody knew about ME. Cared. Wanted me
to breathe, to talk, to live.

Those seven words, how can I ever forget them! *Oral,
God is going to heal you.* Jewel knew. Perhaps unconsciously
I knew too. But it took her words to awaken this knowledge

within me. For the first time, I WANTED GOD TO BE MINE. I WANTED TO CONFESS MY SINS TO HIM AND PLEAD FOR FORGIVENESS. I WANTED PEACE IN MY SOUL . . . I WANTED THE LORD . . . I WANTED EVERYTHING HE STOOD FOR.

THE DAY GOD BECAME REAL TO ME

I heard myself sobbing and asked God to have mercy on me, a sinner. I told Him I had been wrong in putting Him out of my life. I asked Him to forgive me and make me a new person.

How can I describe it, the feeling of His presence that started at my feet and swept up through me – a joy that almost burst my emotions, a peace that stilled the anxiety and fear in my heart, a knowing that my sins were forgiven and I was new inside. Jesus Christ was closer to me than my breath!

Taking my parents in my arms I cried, "Jesus Christ has come into my heart. He's saved me; He's given me salvation. Today God has become real to me!" I asked for the Bible and began reading, and God's Word came alive to me. In fact, Bible verses I had learned in church as a little boy came back to me.

Then two words of Jesus leaped out at me, words I had said in Sunday school when the teacher suddenly called on each of us to recite a verse in the Bible, and I would always say, "JESUS WEPT," because it was a verse I could always remember. But I laughed when I said it and so did the other children, for they knew I was saying it because it was so easy to remember.

BUT NOW, as Christ had come into my heart and saved me, *JESUS WEPT* took on a new meaning. I began to weep myself for I realized why He wept; something was wrong; He was concerned about it; He had come to raise people up, and He had raised up my soul into salvation!

HE SAT WHERE I SAT...
HE FELT WHAT I FELT

That's what *Jesus wept* meant to me. The dawning that Jesus Christ was IN me, along with Jewel's promise that God was going to heal me, opened my eyes to THE MIRACLE OF ABUNDANT LIFE.

From that time on the devil was never able to take away the faith that I found was in my heart.

Papa, Mamma, and Jewel had a conference and agreed that God was able to heal me. They believed He was going to heal me.

Shortly thereafter my eldest brother visited me. "Get up, Oral," Elmer said, "I'm taking you to a revival meeting where a man is praying for the sick."

"I can't get up," I said, "I haven't been able to walk in months."

"I'll carry you," he said, and dressed me and put me on a mattress in the back seat of the car he was driving. As we drove to the meeting and Elmer was telling my parents of the miracles he had seen through God's healing power, I listened. Then a Voice deep inside me spoke, "Son, I am going to heal you and you are to take MY healing power to your generation."

MY REASON FOR BEING

This was the first time I knew my reason for being. God had a purpose for me and it was to bring His healing power to people who were being hindered and cut down in life.

When the evangelist prayed for me that night he prayed in the name of the "mighty Jesus of Nazareth," and commanded, "You foul sickness, come out of this boy!"

I REMEMBER IT LIKE IT WAS YESTERDAY.

At first, there was a warmth like warm water coming over me. It went into my lungs. I'd been breathing off the top of my lungs because if I didn't I would hemorrhage. But I took a deep breath and I could breathe all the way down. I knew that a miracle was starting. The minister talked to me a moment and had me to talk back, and I talked without stammering.

In a few moments' time I was standing straight and tall. I was breathing down deep. I was talking. I was a healed man and in my heart God's voice was ringing:

"Son, I am healing you and you are to take
MY healing power to your generation."

On the way home that night, I became quiet and subdued. It seemed that I had been in a mighty rain and wind, and now the storm was over. Things were quiet. I began to realize that I was in another world. Yes, I was still on this earth but it was not the same world that I had been living in. The world of hopelessness had been banished from my life.

I had been saved . . . now Christ was Lord of my life.

I had been very ill . . . now I was becoming a whole person.

I had been in the shadow of death . . . now I was going to live in the brightness of God's presence, His health and His strength.

I had been away from God . . . now my life was starting to be directed by God. I had received His command to take the message of Christ's healing power to the people of my generation.

Deep within myself, I knew I had to go to the whole world and tell what God had done for me.

HEALING IS IN EVERYTHING I DO

Because I found Christ at the point of my need of salvation and at the point of my need of physical healing, I first thought healing was more or less for the spiritual and physical only. Over the years in experiencing God's healing power flowing through me, it directed me to people with all kinds of needs — so much so, that soon I saw sickness as a more encompassing negative power in a person or family. In other words, I began to understand from God's point of view that anything wrong in a person's life was a form of illness — whether it was a disease, or a spiritual need, or bills piling up and no money to pay, or trouble in the marriage, or alienation in the family or between friends, or fear, or feelings of inadequacy, or worry, or frustration, or inner conflicts, or dreams wrecked. Sickness was anything that was putting the light out in a human life. So gradually the way I prayed took on this deeper meaning, and I began to pray for the healing of the whole man — the person — and what was wrong in his life that was making him less of a person.

I have carried this over into building a university which includes education, but also includes creating conditions for the healing of the totality of man. To keep this healing concept at the center of all we do, we are limiting our enrollment to 3,000 and creating a family relationship where we are all interrelated, and where we can "touch and agree" so that God will be in our midst in His loving healing presence. I carry the "touch-and-agree" concept of healing over into our television and radio work too, making it the heart of that moment of contact between me and the viewer or listener — so that as we "touch one another and pray for one another" it produces the elements in which God may come forth in His healing power. It is working in thousands of people. It's the most thrilling time of my life and ministry.

Now for more than 27 years I have gone across this nation, and on all the continents, with the message that miracles still happen today. It hasn't always been easy. I remember one night a friend watched me washing my hands after praying for hundreds of people. (Many times I had to disinfect my hands because of the odor on them from certain types of diseases people had.) But it was more than this that he saw. I was involved with them at the point of their need. He said, "How can you go through this day after day? How can you endure it?"

And I said, "BECAUSE I HAVE BEEN THERE. Jesus healed me and I KNOW THE JOY OF A MIRACLE."

As he looked at me, still not comprehending, I said, "It's more than that. God has called me. His calling is part of my being. It's my reason for living. What I do, I have to do. For me, there's no other way."

IF YOU NEED A MIRACLE I WANT YOU TO REMEMBER THIS...

Another thing I have discovered is that a miracle is not something for nothing. So many people inadvertently think this. I've learned you've got to give God something to work with . . . you've got to give God a seed, a seed of faith (Matthew 17:20). A miracle is the same as a harvest, and a harvest always comes from seed planted. My personal miracle began when Jewel gave to me of her faith . . . when she put this seed into my life by giving me those seven words that opened my understanding of God, "Oral, God is going to heal you."

My parents also planted seeds of concern and faith in caring for me and encouraging me to believe God for a miracle. My brother borrowed a car so he could take me to a service to receive prayer for healing. That was a great seed of faith in my behalf. Finally, I had to respond; I had to open up inside myself and give of my love and faith. My miracle happened because seed was planted, and it was seed planted FIRST. The Bible says:

He (God) that ministers seed to the sower . . .
and multiplies your seed sown . . .

What does God multiply??? THE SEED SOWN. The seed has to be given FIRST. We cannot say, "If God gives me a harvest then I'll take some of His seed and give it to Him." No! We have to start where we are . . . and give something of what we have. That is, we plant FIRST. We give it as the seed we sow whether it is our love, our concern, our time, our money — whatever we give, we give it as the seed we sow. Then God multiplies the seed we sow back to us in the form of a need we have. God gives the harvest or the miracle.

Long before I thought about God and had alienated myself from both God and my parents, my family was putting in the seeds of their faith and love for me. They were focusing all this on God, asking Him for help, believing He would help, and expecting a miracle. Finally, I had to act on my own — to make my decision, my commitment. To open up my inner being and deliberately turn to God. To give of myself to Him, to faith, to the possibility of a miracle happening *to me*, Oral Roberts.

Perhaps this is why I told Merv Griffin the greatest miracle I ever saw was my own *personal miracle* . . . because it happened to me. Perhaps that is also why I am able to help so many others. I know it happened to me; therefore, I know there's the very real possibility it can happen to anyone.

Here is where it all started — at our church in Enid, Oklahoma.

CHAPTER TWO

THE FIRST MIRACLE
I HELPED ANOTHER PERSON RECEIVE

and the knowing it brought to me
that a miracle could happen to
every person in my generation — in the now!

IN 1947 I CAME TO THE CROSSROADS of my life. As a young pastor and college student, I had to have some answers that neither my church nor my college was giving me. I began a study of the Bible as I never had before. My Bible was usually open to the Four Gospels and the book of Acts in the New Testament. Often I studied these Scriptures on my knees. As I read the Gospels and the Acts . . .

I saw how Jesus cared for people and had compassion and healed them.

I saw that Jesus had come in the likeness of man and in the likeness of God — Son of God, Son of man. My mind couldn't understand it but my spirit could.

I saw that Jesus had come to show us what God is like . . . that God is not against people — God is *for* people!

I saw that Jesus came to DELIVER AND HEAL THE PEOPLE . . . to set them free . . . to give them abundant life *in the now* of their existence!!!

I saw that Jesus was always IN THE NOW — the same yesterday, today and forever.

I saw that He was in the *now* of my generation, and He wanted to continue to give men life more abundantly, to really be the Source of their lives and to supply all their needs.

I saw that He actually sat where we sit, He feels what we feel, and is at the point of the need of each human being.

I saw that it is at the point of your need where you look for Him and where you will find Him.

This thrilled and excited me; I felt I would burst inside if I didn't share it. Strangely enough, this brought a deep *dissatisfaction* in my life.

On the one hand I was studying in the university, supposedly studying truth, learning how to ask questions. On the other hand I was a Christian . . . a young pastor preaching the Word of God. I saw the gap between what I saw Jesus Christ *to be in the now* and what I saw people's understanding of Him to be. I saw what Jesus had done 2,000 years ago and was present to do in my generation, and what scant knowledge we had that He would actually do the same things, only greater, if we saw Him as He is, and would believe.

I began to ask questions:

Why aren't we more like Jesus?

Why don't we heal the people as He did?

Why are we not concerned about the total man — his soul, mind, body, all of his needs . . . the whole of his existence as well as his future in eternity?

Why aren't we concerned about the individual as he lives on earth facing life as it really is?

I shared these thoughts with some people but got no answers. I was shut up in the silence of my own heart . . . trying to understand this man Jesus of Nazareth . . . and seeking to find ways to break out with the greatest news of all:

JESUS CHRIST IS ALIVE!
HE'S IN THE NOW! HE WANTS TO HEAL YOU!

One night I had a dream. In that dream God let me see people, much as He SEES them . . . and HEARS them . . . and FEELS them. I saw that EVERYBODY HAS A NEED. EVERYBODY IS SICK IN SOME WAY. I saw that sickness is disharmony:

> If something is wrong in the soul, to that extent the man is sick.
>
> If something is wrong in the mind, to that extent the man is sick.
>
> If something is wrong in the body, to that extent the man is sick.
>
> If something is wrong in his family that touches his own life a man is often thrown out of rhythm and balance with his own life, and to that extent the man is sick.
>
> If something is wrong financially, to that extent the man is sick.
>
> If something is wrong in any way, in any part of his existence, to that extent he is sick.

In this way, I SAW THE SICKNESS OF PEOPLE AND . . . OH . . . IT TURNED ME ON TO WHAT JESUS CHRIST IS ALL ABOUT . . . THAT HE IS IN THE WORLD TO TOUCH PEOPLE AT THE POINT OF THEIR NEED. And I was in the world with His message of His healing power.

My wife Evelyn said, "Oral, you've been getting up at night and walking the floor. What's wrong?"

"The cause of my being so upset at this time is a dream God has been giving me," I told her. "It has been the same dream night after night and it devastates me."

"What is the dream, Oral?" she asked.

"I dream that God shows me mankind as He sees them and as He hears them. What I see and hear takes my breath away."

"Well, what do they look like?" she asked me.

"Have you ever gone into a hospital and heard the moans and groans of people really ill? Have you ever seen a person so sick with his problems and torments that he is beside himself? Have you ever seen a human being so down in his spirit it's like life is over for him? That is how I'm seeing people now. I did not know it before but everybody is sick in some way. They must have healing from God."

I could say no more for my dream had become too real as I retold it. Evelyn took me into her arms and we cried together.

That night I began to grow up to the work God had made for me.

I was 29½ years old.

But I was a man. I was finally ready to answer the calling of God. I knew WHAT God wanted me to do but I didn't know HOW. But the HOW would never have been answered if I had not had this deep feeling inside that NOW was God's time for me to begin.

I looked at Evelyn and said, "Honey, I have this knowing inside me that God wants me to follow Jesus the way He really is . . . to carry His compassion for people . . . to try to bring His healing power to the people . . . but I don't know HOW."

Slowly and thoughtfully she said, "Oral, I've had a feeling from the very beginning of our marriage that God has His hand on you — and I believe you DO know what you have to do . . ."

God was speaking through her and I felt it. I felt God directing me to enter into a fast and to spend time in meditation and prayer. It wouldn't be easy because I was carrying 16 hours in college, pastoring a church, and taking care of my young family. However, there was a drive in my soul which I could not explain. It burned in me like a fire; it blew through me like a wind; it pounded me like a hammer; night and day it roared in my mind. I could not get away from it.

One day I went to my little church study and opened my Bible to the book of Acts. I read about the miracles until the possibility of this happening in the now literally caused me to fall to the floor. There on my face before God I began talking to God, saying things like this: "God, You spoke to people in the Bible. You had to speak to the people in the Bible or they couldn't have written it. You've spoken to men throughout the ages. You spoke to me 12 years ago that You were going to heal me and that I was to take Your healing power to my generation . . . now will You speak to me again? Will You tell me what I am . . . who I am . . . what I'm to do with my life . . . how I am to carry out the calling that You have given me?"

It seemed like I was a tiny speck in the universe. I was reaching up to God. I didn't even know if I was being heard but my heart was pounding and saying, "Speak to me, Lord." And He did speak. Later I felt these words deep within me:

"FROM THIS HOUR YOU WILL HAVE MY POWER TO HEAL THE SICK, TO DETECT THE

PRESENCE OF DEMONS, TO KNOW THEIR NUMBER AND THEIR NAME AND TO HAVE MY POWER TO CAST THEM OUT."

I still didn't understand these words completely but I knew that I had heard from GOD and that if I ever did any of these things it would be by *His power*.

I drove home and told Evelyn to cook a meal for me. As we ate, we laughed and cried and talked and rejoiced. We knew it was a new day!!!

Then I said, "Evelyn, we've got to be sure. It's easy to say that God is directing but it has to work in the practical realities of everyday life."

I was thinking of Jesus' words, "Thy will be done in earth, as it is in heaven" (Matthew 6:10).

So I decided to prove to myself that God had truly spoken to me here "in this earth." So I secured the use of an auditorium in downtown Enid at 2 p.m. the following Sunday and announced a service and invited the people to come for my message and prayer. I said, "God, if I really heard Your voice and I'm to do what You've asked me to do, then . . .

(1) Give me an audience of at least 1,000 people (I had been preaching to a congregation of less than 200).

(2) Supply the financial costs in an honorable way.

(3) Heal the people by divine power so conclusively that they, as well as I, will know I am called of God to carry on this ministry of Your healing power!!

I promised God, "If You will grant these three things I will resign my pastorate and enter immediately into evangelistic crusades; I will go to the people at the point of their needs."

As I looked forward to this critical meeting, I was suddenly faced with an overwhelming sense of failure. For 2 days I wrestled with this awful question. It pounded in my breast. What if I fail? What if I fail? Suddenly, very clearly, God said, *You have already done that.*

I was shocked to the depths of my spirit. Then slowly I realized what He meant. My mediocre preaching — my following the pattern of many other preachers — this was failure in God's sight when compared to the ministry I should have had. When God gently pointed out my failure, He also gave the finest opportunity I had ever faced — *I COULD START OVER!* I could start over where I was in that moment. I didn't have to go to another city for the first meeting, I could do it at home where I was best known and where it would be the hardest. A deep peace settled over me.

But I was still scared when the day arrived. I was so scared that I couldn't eat. It was Sunday. Some of the church people joined me. At 2 o'clock we went downtown to the auditorium.

The custodian met me at the door and said, "Mr. Roberts, there are 1,200 people here."

"Thank God," I said to myself, "condition number one is settled ..."

Later we received the offering to pay the rent on the building, which was $160.00. This was a big amount in those days to a young preacher. When it was counted the offering was $163.03 — $3.03 over. That was the plus. God was bringing in the miracle.

After I preached and began to pray for the people God began to bring His healing power to the needs of the people.

The first person I prayed for was a German woman. She had a bent and crippled hand which had been like that for 38 years. She spoke in broken English and when God healed her hand she cried at the top of her voice, "I'm healed!!! I'm healed!!!" People saw her and were broken up by it.

That afternoon I prayed for the unsaved and for the sick from about 3 until 6 o'clock. Soon there wasn't a dry thread of clothing on my body. But when I walked out of that building that evening . . .

I knew that Jesus Christ had come forth from the Gospels and the Acts of the apostles like a hurricane into a young man's heart.

I saw a world that was hurting and I wanted to go to it.

I wanted to hug people — to touch them. I wanted to love them and tell them that Jesus of Nazareth loved them.

A knowing welled up within me that day — a knowing of God's NOWNESS. A knowing of God's will and purpose for my life. A knowing I was called of God to minister His miracle power to my generation. A knowing I was born for this cause.

Something even more important happened as I walked out of the auditorium that evening.

God had actually worked through me to help another receive a healing and the impact of it had touched 1,200 other human beings. It was a pebble thrown in the pool, causing little ripples at first then those ripples getting wider and wider until they encompassed the whole pool. What happened there could happen to every person in my generation!

First, the great miracle was the one that had happened to me. The second was one happening through me to another person and its results affecting 1,200 others; and not the least, its effect upon me and the way I would in the future see the possibility of a miracle happening in every other fellow human being.

I had come alive from my own illness and defeat, and I had come alive to God doing the same for millions of others.

This second miracle couldn't have happened without the first. But the first could only be meaningful through the second miracle — the knowing that it can happen to every person in my generation.

A new phrase came to my life:

GOD IS A GOOD GOD!

It was a statement I would make thousands of times until it would become a household word.

THE SECOND MIRACLE AND YOU

You know, nothing becomes real to you until you experience it for yourself. You will never know Christ's healing power until it happens to you.

You probably don't have the same illness I had, or the affliction the woman had in my first healing service. But like me, and everyone else, you become ill in some way from time to time. In fact, to the extent you face problems that throw you off balance; or make you afraid; or cause you to hurt; or frustrate you; or get you down, you are sick — and so am I and everyone else. You know this is true because you are experiencing it.

Well, healing can be experienced to the same extent you are experiencing any of these problems. Only then will you know for sure God performs miracles. You may believe that you know without a miracle happening to you but you will only really KNOW when you experience a miracle yourself.

I hear these things from so many people as they write me:

"Oral Roberts, why has this happened to me? What have I done to deserve it?" . . . and

"Oral Roberts, who am I to deserve a miracle from God? He is too busy to be thinking about me. Why should He be concerned about me?"

I know exactly how you feel. It's the way I felt, and occasionally I feel that way again.

All I can say is what I know. Not hearsay, not intellectual assent, not what I merely hope for — but what I KNOW.

I know God exists and that He loves you.

I know He is very concerned for you and wants to help you, even to giving you a miracle.

I know that God is at the point of your need, and if, when you hurt the most, you look for Him you will find He is there, and He is there with miracles in His hands.

I know you have faith — God put it in every person's heart (Romans 12:3) and He put it in yours — and that you can put in a seed of faith toward God now.

You may ask, "Oral Roberts, how do you know these things concerning God and me?"

I can only say from the depths of my heart that I know that I know that I know that I know!

The Memorial Auditorium in Chanute, Kansas, where God gave us a miracle through my wife Evelyn that kept me from quitting this ministry.

CHAPTER THREE

THE MIRACLE THROUGH EVELYN THAT KEPT ME FROM QUITTING THIS MINISTRY

THERE WAS A TIME when it seemed that Evelyn and I were growing apart. I was completely absorbed in my rapidly growing ministry. And Evelyn was busy with our four small children. She was trying to be both mother and father since I was gone as much as 9 months out of the year. It was not that we loved each other any less. We were just growing apart — learning to live without "needing" each other.

One evening after Evelyn had tucked the children in bed she came back to the living room and picked up a book to read when I said, "Wait a minute, Evelyn. I want to talk . . ." She looked at me a little puzzled and said, "About what?"

"Well," I answered, "I think we are growing apart."

"What are you saying . . .?" she exclaimed. "I love you as much as ever and I know you love me. I think we have a perfectly normal life, except that you have to travel and I have to be at home with the children. I know we're physically separated a lot but we still love each other and have a normal life."

I said, "That's just it, Evelyn. I don't want us to have just a *normal life*. That isn't enough for us. I want us always to *need* each other — to *always* be *sweethearts*."

She thought a moment and then said, "I think I see what you mean, Oral. I guess we are just so busy doing the good things and the right things that we are taking each other for granted."

That night as we prayed together we dedicated ourselves to each other anew and asked the Lord to help us always to be one together, and one in Him and in our ministry. And as we prayed, it was like the Lord wrapped us together in His great love. It was as though there had never been a gap. After 35 years of marriage we are still sweethearts and expect to be right on.

In fact, Evelyn and I are more than sweethearts. She plays a dynamic part in this ministry of deliverance.

EVELYN'S MIRACLE FOR ME

I remember one time in the very early part of our ministry when I closed my Bible, walked away, and said, "I'm through . . ."

It was November 1947. I was preaching a crusade in a city auditorium in Kansas. People were coming to the crusade from a three-state area. There was a great spirit in the meetings and the people were responding to the invitation to accept Christ as Savior and Lord, and many were receiving healing for their illnesses and problems. There was only one thing wrong — the crusade expenses were not being met. As we neared the close of the crusade the money for the rent of the auditorium was not in hand, and I became very distressed. There had been times before this when Evelyn and I had done without in order to pay the bills in connection with our ministry.

The mistake I made this time was to brood and worry instead of looking to God, the Source of my TOTAL supply.

(This of course was before I really understood the miracle of Seed-Faith.)

I took it as a personal failure of my ability to trust God. I allowed it to develop into a matter between God and me. The more I thought about the rent coming due and not having enough funds on hand to pay it, the more disturbed I became. I felt if I could not trust God for finances, how could I trust him for souls to be saved and the sick to be healed? If the Lord had really sent me to the people with the message of His healing and delivering power, I reasoned, and if He expected me to be His instrument, I had every right to expect sufficient funds to be raised to meet the obligations incurred by the ministry. I could not bear to think of closing the crusade and leaving the city with the bills unpaid. I would sell every personal thing I had — my car, my clothes, everything if need be to pay those bills. Anything less was a contradiction to all I was and stood for in integrity and faith.

In spite of my thoughts, nothing changed. The crowds were large and enthusiastic, the spirit was high, and the results were miraculous. Still, we fell further behind in the crusade budget.

One evening I was waiting behind the curtain to be announced to preach. My brother Vaden was standing near me. All at once something broke within me and I said to him, "I am through."

He said, "What's wrong?"

I said, "I don't have the faith and God is not helping me."

He said, "Well, Oral, this is a wonderful crusade."

I said, "Yes, but we can't pay the bills, and you know that Papa always taught us to be honest and pay our debts."

I said, "Vaden, I have done everything I know to do. I have preached the gospel, prayed for the sick, and people have come to God. Now we can't even pay the rent on this building. I can't continue and be honest.

"I am through.

It is all over.

I am going home."

Vaden left and soon returned with Evelyn. She was as white as a sheet. She knew when I said something I meant it. And there behind the curtain she put her arms around me and said, "Oral, I know it's hard but you can't quit now. The services are too good and the people are turning more to your ministry every day."

"Evelyn, you know my vow. You and I both promised God that we would never touch the gold or the glory, but we have to have enough to meet our budget. You know it, and I know it. I have prayed to God but He has not heard me. If I am to continue in this ministry God will meet our needs. If not, I am going home."

She said, "Oral, why don't you go out there and tell the crowd how you feel? Maybe they will do more."

I said, "No. God knows my needs. If I can't trust Him for this, how can I trust Him for the other things?"

She said, "Aren't you going to preach tonight?"

I said, "No, it's all over."

She and Vaden left. Pretty soon I heard her talking to the crowd. For a moment it startled me. She had never done this before. In fact, she always said, "When I stand up in front of an audience my mind sits down." But this time she was really talking.

I looked through the curtains. The people were looking at each other and wondering what the evangelist's wife was doing in the pulpit. Moving over to where I could see, as well as hear, I heard her say:

"Friends, you don't know what it means for me to stand up here tonight in my husband's place. And I am sure you don't know him as I do. He has come here by faith. No one is responsible for the financial needs to be met except him and God. He has preached and prayed for you and your loved ones each evening, but tonight he feels like quitting. Some of you have not realized your responsibility in supporting this ministry. We can't even pay the rent on the building. Whatever you may think of Oral, there is this about him that you must know. He is honest and if he cannot pay the rent he will not go on. He will not blame you. He will take it as a sign that God does not want him to continue his ministry, and he will stop. *I know God has called him and that he must continue to obey God. I am asking you to help him. Together we can save this ministry.*"

As she spoke, big tears splashed down her face, and I felt smaller and smaller.

"What kind of a man am I," I asked myself, "who would quit when the going gets tough? This is probably a very little trial compared to what I will face in the future." (Little did I realize at that moment how really *big* problems can get!)

These and other questions raced through my mind. Still, I could not change my mind. It was a point of integrity. God had called me, and my needs had to be met. I had heard of others leaving unpaid bills behind, bringing a reproach on the ministry, but I would either pay the bills or I would not preach.

I heard Evelyn say, "Maybe some of you don't know we are in need. Perhaps you are waiting for my husband to say more about it. He won't say any more about it. He won't say any more, for his trust is in God. Now I'm going to do something I've never done in my life. I want some man here to lend me his hat, and I'm going to take a freewill offering for the rent."

Several men volunteered their hats. Evelyn selected a big-brimmed, black one. Holding the hat close to her, she bowed her head and prayed. I could tell she was embarrassed. Still, she was determined to save my ministry. She said:

"All right, now, the Lord and you must help us. Not just for people here who have need of healing, but for people in other places and lands. I am coming among you to pass the hat. I ask God to help you do your part and to bless you for helping us."

Oh, how small my faith was that night. I did not expect Evelyn to succeed. It seemed I had swung too far from the shore and it was time I was striking for home. The devil whispered, "Well, you have sunk pretty low. When you have to let your wife take the offering, it's time you gave up."

Listening to the devil and knowing Evelyn felt like dropping through the floor, I knew I was near total defeat. I actually was blaming God. The truth was that by not remembering who is the Source for my TOTAL supply I was letting God down.

We needed only $300 to finish paying the auditorium rent. But because we didn't have $300 it was as large in my mind as a sum ten times larger. It was at this moment that the hand of the Lord touched me. This is a sensation that is difficult to put into words, but I always know and recognize it when it comes to me. It is this touch that changes me from Oral Roberts, just an average human being, to a God-anointed man.

Suddenly a man stood up in the audience and asked Evelyn for permission to say a word. He was a Jewish businessman who had been attending the services and we had taken a meal in his home. He had been deeply impressed with the crusade and we were praying for him. He said:

"Folks, you all know me. I am not a Christian; but if I ever am, these people (gesturing toward the platform) have what I want. I have some money I owe the Lord. I'm starting this offering with $20."

Evelyn just stood there and waited. Suddenly a large red-haired woman stood and said, "I'm ashamed of every one in this audience, especially of myself. I'm the mother of several children. We have lots of needs and the Lord has helped us get many of these needs met through His servant Oral Roberts. Now you listen to me; I want every one of you to do what I'm going to do." Then she opened her purse, pulled out a worn dollar bill, put it in the hat, and sat down. In a few moments people were standing and saying, "Mrs. Roberts, bring that hat over here."

As Evelyn went through the crowd, holding out the black hat with the big western brim, I was thoroughly ashamed of myself. When she had finished with the offering, I had the courage at last to step to the platform. I was conscious that every eye was upon me. I had no idea whether enough had been raised to meet the rent. A new feeling was taking possession of me. My wife had done something few wives would have had courage to do for their husbands. I knew she had not done this only for me. A team of wild horses could not have pulled her up there. She had willingly gone before the people because she felt the ministry, which she knew God had given me, was endangered. I was proud of her and ashamed of myself for letting doubt and fear creep into my mind.

When the need was fully met, I knew that it was an answer from God to me personally. It was also a gentle rebuke. When I stepped forward to take over the service I made no reference whatever to what Evelyn had done, feeling that I could only atone for it by taking my Bible and again preaching the gospel and praying for the people. I read my text and began to preach. I tell you I felt like a Niagara of power released. I knew that the tide had changed. This meeting ended with a packed house and with the audience standing en masse, urging us to return for another crusade.

I am sure that when God gives out the credit for the success of this crusade, more of it will be due my wife than to me. The thing she did that night meant more to me than raising the funds to pay the bills. It proved to me again that Evelyn was my helpmeet — truly a gift from God . . . and He had used Evelyn in a miracle that saved this ministry.

WHEN YOU ARE THREATENED

There just isn't any way to get through life without having your very existence threatened. And it's strange how something like unpaid rent can become such a great threat.

The fact is the devil knows where you are vulnerable, your weakest point. He hits you there and keeps on hitting.

Jesus called this "facing a mountain . . ." Mountains come in different sizes and shapes and in Jesus' reference they refer to the problems and needs you face, the things which appear impossible to you. But He is so real, so compassionate, so understanding, AND so practical that He both recognizes the mountain being there and the way to get it removed. What it is He promises is in the MIRACLE OF SEED-FAITH. In Matthew 17:20, Jesus says:

If ye have faith as a grain of mustard
seed, ye shall say unto this mountain,
Remove hence to yonder place; and it
shall remove; and nothing shall be
impossible unto you.

As I stood fearing and trembling over the bills there in the crusade, ready to give up and walk out, I could have completely failed and I wouldn't be writing this book. Had not Evelyn made her faith as a seed planted, if she hadn't given of herself that evening, even though she was horribly embarrassed to do it, then no seed would have been planted . . . and there would have been no harvest — which is to say, since harvest and miracles mean the same thing in Bible terms, there would have been NO MIRACLE . . . no miracle, and Oral Roberts would have "chickened out."

A seed of faith is what you give God to work with IN THE SAME WAY A FARMER GIVES SEED TO THE EARTH TO WORK WITH TO BRING FORTH A HARVEST. And you've got to give a seed to match your need.

Well, Evelyn did, and I finally did, and God gave the harvest (THE MIRACLE).

What is in your life that you are threatened with? Is it like a mountain you can't climb?

Somebody in your household can do something that will be in harmony with the 3 Miracle Keys of Seed-Faith that our Lord has given us. Maybe you can, or something within you can. Just as Evelyn had to swallow her pride and step forth and sow a seed of faith, you can do it.

When I think of how only 6 months after this ministry started my fear could have ended it all, I still tremble a little. All those millions I've ministred to in crusades, on radio, on television, in my writings, the Oral Roberts University — none of this would have happened if Evelyn, my darling wife, had not in that pressure-packed moment let God use her in a miracle that saved this ministry.

Oh, the wonder of what a wife with faith in God can do for her husband!

This is what was left of our tent after the Amarillo storm.

CHAPTER FOUR

THE MIRACLE THAT SAVED 7,000 FROM DEATH

(An account of the tent crusades, and of the escape of 7,000 people from a storm that destroyed the big tent)

I SOMETIMES THINK ABOUT MY CRUSADES in the big "Tent Cathedral" during the late '40s, through the '50s and most of the '60s. Although the way I'm carrying on this ministry today is reaching many times more now, yet during those years that was God's method for me to reach the people. To stand before 10,000 seated, and thousands more standing around at the edge of the tent was a thrill beyond description. Each was a living, breathing human being to me — one I could see, feel, and reach out to with everything in me.

The first tent was 220 by 180 feet — the last was 460 by 220 feet, about three times the size of a football field. Eight stainless steel trailers pulled by eight huge trucks transported the big canvas, the poles, platform, and thousands of portable seats — it was a movable auditorium that could be set up in one day in any sizable city in the nation. To drive up to it and see it packed night after night, to witness the drama of the hundreds coming down the aisles to accept Christ, or the hundreds coming in the "healing lines" in full public view — the successes and failures right before your eyes — was an experience several million people will never forget. Certainly, I won't.

The first tent in 1948 accommodated 3,000 seats inside, and each one became progressively larger, seating 4,500, 7,000, 10,000, 12,000 — not counting those who stood in deep lines surrounding the tent. Many times the police estimated as many outside as there were seated inside.

I recall that one man was asked how he enjoyed the meeting. He said, "Oh, I couldn't get a seat but I sure had a great place to stand!"

What he didn't say was he stood 4 solid hours! He had to get there an hour early to find a place to stand and he remained for the entire service which lasted 3 hours.

If those big tents could talk they would, I believe, tell of miracle after miracle after miracle — many of which I will never know about until we get to heaven.

But there was one great miracle that I'll never forget as long as I live. It happened in the Amarillo, Texas Crusade. I call it "The night God rode with us." At that time the tent seated 7,000. Here's what happened.

In September 1950 we took the big tent to Amarillo, Texas. The Amarillo Crusade was great. More than 2,450 souls were saved. The miracles of healing were outstanding and people were moved with the presence and power of the Lord.

On the tenth night, a storm struck. The winds came roaring in out of the northwest. I was standing at the pulpit when suddenly the lights went out. I shouted, "Everyone stay seated and keep your mind on God!" They did. In the flash of lightning I saw the entire tent begin to lift toward the sky — it looked like billows of light — then begin to settle, floating down slowly.

"Oh, Lord, save the 7,000 people from harm!" I prayed.

It seemed as if a thousand invisible hands took control of the situation.

I remember a statement I had made in one of my sermons during the meeting. I said, "The storms of life come to everybody — to the saved and unsaved, to those who live in God's will and to those who don't. The only difference is that Jesus is in the Christian's boat, just like He was with the disciples (Luke 8:22-25), and that makes all the difference in the world."

I felt that God was riding with us that night. The lightning flashed all around us and the winds roared like a freight train. The next thing I knew, the rear of the tent lifted over my head and I felt myself falling backward. I said, "Lord, this is it." I was laid down very gently on the lower section of the platform as if by an invisible hand. I still had the microphone in my hands. I was not hurt. Then I heard several hundred people singing. A man near me began to praise the Lord. I climbed back to the main platform which was still intact.

I looked back at the crowd. The aluminum poles were gently lowering toward the people on the chairs. The big 1,000-pound steel center poles were inching toward the ground. A part of the tent draped over the chairs and I saw people crawling out from under the tattered tent, fighting canvas off their heads. *No one panicked.*

I believe there were angels in that tent that night.

Every person came out alive. About fifty people were slightly hurt, but none seriously.

I ran from group to group praying with people and praising God for our safety. It was several minutes before I realized that I did not know where my wife and baby were. Evelyn had come to the meeting with Richard. (He was 2 years old at the time.) I began to call, "Evelyn, Evelyn." I came back out and met Vaden, my brother. He shouted,

"Oral, she and Richard are all right. They are under the platform." I got them out and into the car.

Meanwhile the hail was really coming down. People had chairs over their heads to protect them.

The firemen got there, went through the tent, and announced that no one was left under it. A policeman rushed up to me and said, "Reverend Roberts, this is the most miraculous thing I have ever seen."

Around midnight Evelyn and I got to our room. We turned on the radio. Fifty people were reported injured, but none seriously hurt. I thanked God.

Already the media was proclaiming it a miracle. They recalled the circus tent fire in Hartford, Connecticut, where more than 100 people were killed and hundreds injured, and now they were marveling. More than 7,000 people had been under our tent; every one of them escaped. The reporters found me. I told them how it happened. One was almost in tears. "Brother Roberts," he said, "God was there." The next morning the Amarillo Times crowded the war news off the front page and ran a blazing headline: ESCAPE OF 7,000 CALLED MIRACLE.

The next day I went out to see the wreckage. Poles and ripped canvas lay over the chairs. How anybody could have gotten out alive can only be answered by saying, "This is the greatest miracle I have ever seen." One of the insurance men said to me, "Reverend Roberts, the good Lord had His hand over this place last night." He was right. The Lord had given us a miracle. But as I stood there surveying the wreckage and wondering again if I was through, someone ran up with a telegram that was from one of our partners in Colorado. It read:

"DEAR BROTHER ROBERTS:
YOU CAN'T GO UNDER FOR GOING OVER. . . ."

Something leaped in my heart. I looked at the remains of that old tent and for the first time since the storm, tears came to my eyes. I said, "Old tent, you are gone. But I have no regrets. You fought the battle with me and thousands of souls have come to Jesus Christ under your shelter . . ."

Then I said to the Lord, "Lord, I have no regrets. I had nothing when I started 3 years ago but faith. I still have that faith. You protected the lives of 7,000 people in the midst of the storm. No sermon I might have preached could compare with this mighty miracle . . . with Your help, I will begin again — I will secure a bigger tent, one that can withstand the storms . . ."

And this is what we did. I told the people about our plans as I preached on our radio broadcasts. I told them how faith leaped in my heart. I told them how the words of my own sermon came back to me through a telegram: "YOU CAN'T GO UNDER FOR GOING OVER." I told them, "With God's help we're *going over* . . ." and we did.

Twenty-three years later, while teaching my class on THE HOLY SPIRIT IN THE NOW at Oral Roberts University, Dr. Howard Ervin, who is the Chairman of the Department of Theology at ORU, thrilled the class of 2,500 students when he told this story. He said:

"President Roberts, the first sermon I ever heard you preach was on the radio one Sunday morning. It was 'YOU CAN'T GO UNDER FOR GOING OVER.' You were retelling the miracle that came out of the chaos of the Amarillo incident. And at that time, I was a pessimistic Christian. I had not experienced the fullness of the baptism in the Holy Spirit. And even though I was an ordained Baptist minister and pastoring a large church, I could see no hope for the Church — I was, indeed a pessimistic pastor. But as you told this story, I thought, if this man can be optimistic in the midst of chaos, why am I so doubtful? He's got *something* that I just don't have."

Dr. Ervin later found out what I had that he didn't have — it is what I call "the miracle of the prayer language of the Spirit," which I will be discussing in a later chapter in this book. He of course later received this experience. He is a man of great spiritual stature, a man who truly "walks in the Spirit . . . " (Galatians 5:25).

But for a little more interesting background on the destruction of the old tent: In 1950 engineers apparently had not yet been able to construct a tent that could survive a hundred-mile-an-hour wind. So apparently the Lord intended that I would be the testing point.

After our tent went down we met with a group of engineers and came up with a plan for a tent that would stand the storms. It was much larger than we'd ever had before and of course more durable. In fact, they told us that this tent could withstand the winds better than a brick building.

We took them at their word and ordered the tent. And for the next 15 years we used tents for our crusades that would seat up to 12,000. And these tents experienced winds that were even stronger than the Amarillo storm but they were never blown down.

Out of seeming disaster came the seed of an equivalent benefit. And out of it came into my heart a faith that what I was doing was indestructible. Not only was it indestructible — it could not be decreased. It would be MULTIPLIED.

When Lee Braxton, my associate since 1948 and now Chairman of the ORU Board of Regents, heard about the storm, he flew from North Carolina, where he was Mayor of his city, to Amarillo. He came out to the tent site, put his arm around me, and said, "Oral, this ministry has in it the seeds of a worldwide revival. It's going to be bigger and stronger than ever before . . ."

Now anyone who knows me, knows that I ask a lot of questions. And I said to him, "Lee, what do you base that on?"

He said, "I base it upon the fact that when I attended your crusade in Miami, Florida, I saw among the hundreds that were healed a navy captain healed of cancer. I saw a little child run who had never run before. I saw more people converted in one night than I'd seen won to Christ in my whole life. I base it upon the power of God and His call on your life to take this ministry of deliverance to the whole world . . . "

Now Lee had only known me for about a year, so he had to have a lot of faith to make such a statement as we stood there amidst the muddy ruins of that old tent.

CAN GOD GIVE YOU PHYSICAL ESCAPE?

Who is it that has not in the flash of a second found himself facing certain death? Who has not felt fear grab the pit of his stomach when the car swerved on the road, or an airplane bounced in the air, or a car was bearing down on him on a street, or a machine flew apart and he was struck by an object?

Who has not been caught in the elements — a stormy night on land, in air, or on water, or in a building or vehicle?

Who has not faced the prospects of a physical attack by an animal or another human being?

I've been close to death several times during these past 27 years. I could feel the force of it closer than my breath, it seemed. A gun pointed at me, the bullet missing by inches; a mob closing in, spitting in my face, striking my body, clawing at my eyes, my throat. Planes losing a motor, or

49

motors, and crash landing three times. Tires blowing out, the car going out of control, only to be stopped safely as by an invisible guardian. Physical storms — they are real, they are terrifying. Storms of yellow journalism whose purpose is to defame and destroy, lies designed to cripple and kill, financial crises that threatened to wipe you out. Storms of your own stupidity and mistakes when you're saved only because you are straight, sincere, and have something of value to give.

But the storm in Amarillo that night when I saw the miracle that saved 7,000 from what looked like sure death still lives in my mind . . . and that miracle still says "YOU CAN'T GO UNDER FOR GOING OVER!"

On our telecasts I reach out my hand and invite the viewers to do the same as a point of contact when I pray for their needs to be met.

CHAPTER FIVE

THE MIRACLE THAT HAS HELPED THE MOST PEOPLE – THE POINT OF CONTACT

(Through a letter written . . . through touching someone . . . or through something else you DO)

I SUPPOSE ONE-THIRD of the letters I receive are from people who say . . .

> "Oral Roberts, you're always talking about faith . . . you say, 'Have faith in God! Believe God, and miracles will happen!!' Well, what I want to know is HOW . . ."

Others write and say . . .

> "I've tried and I've tried. I've prayed and I've believed but nothing happens!!! What's wrong? Why don't *I* receive a miracle???"

I understand questions like these . . . and they are right and proper. For what good is faith unless you know HOW to use it? Early in my ministry I was frustrated by this problem, too, until God showed me how to help people to release their faith to God and receive miracles. God gave something to my ministry that I call THE POINT OF CONTACT. I call it a miracle because the point of contact has opened the door to miracles for countless thousands.

THE POINT OF CONTACT IS SOMETHING
YOU DO . . . AND WHEN YOU DO IT
YOU RELEASE YOUR FAITH.

I often say when I write a letter to a friend or partner who has asked for prayer:

"This letter is anointed; use it as a point of contact to release your faith to God for your healing."

I especially remember one woman who did this. She had been prayed for many times and had received the laying-on-of-hands but still she was not healed. Then one day she sat down and wrote me a letter. It was just a few lines telling me of her disappointment. She wanted me to read her letter, to offer a prayer for her, and to write her back telling her that I had done so. She said:

"I've come to the place I am no longer looking to you or to any other person, just the Lord."

(She had evidently learned Miracle Key No. 1 of Seed-Faith: Look to God, the Source of your total supply, because GOD is the Source of ALL healing.)

Well, of course I read her letter, I prayed, and I wrote her back. In my letter to her, I said:

"As I pray I feel God's power going through me; therefore, this letter has His Spirit upon it. Lay it on your body as a point of contact, let your faith go to God, AND BE HEALED IN JESUS' NAME."

In just a short time there came back a three-page letter full of praises to God. She told me how she had read my letter, and as she held the letter in her hand she said to the Lord:

"Your Spirit is in Oral Roberts; I feel it in this letter. As I place this letter on my body I am expecting You to give me a miracle of healing."

Then she said:

"Something that felt like a warm liquid started flowing through my entire being. I felt strength, well-being, joy. I knew from that moment that God was healing me . . . and He did."

I thought, Lord, what this woman did, others can do if they will just look to YOU, the Source of all healing power. I believe this with all my heart.

The point of contact is something YOU DO. Oh, I want to stress that. It's something YOU do. It is simply like going over to the light switch. Now the light switch is connected to the powerhouse but you are not going to turn the power-house on. You are going to turn the switch on . . . and the switch is the point of contact. You flip on the light switch and things begin to happen. The current is released from the powerhouse and it begins to flow down the line and the lights come on. Well, now, God is the Source of all healing. But we're not going to turn God on.

GOD IS ALREADY TURNED ON TOWARD US

We are turned on to lots of things in this world but are we turned on to God? That's the big question. The Bible says, "I am the Lord that healeth thee" (Exodus 15:26). Let's get turned on to God. Let's flip that switch of faith to bring His healing power into our lives. Let's DO something — let's get the point of contact to working for us.

Now your point of contact may be writing a letter to me. It may be laying your hand on my letter to you . . . or joining hands with someone at the close of the radio or television program . . . or touching yourself when I pray . . . or launching out with a business venture . . . OR DOING WHATEVER YOU HAVE TO DO TO RELEASE YOUR FAITH. Just remember when you do it . . .

THE POINT OF CONTACT FOCUSES YOUR FAITH ON GOD

One of my associates, Collins Steele, who has been with us for many years, had an accident and hurt his back. It got so bad that he couldn't stand the pain. No matter what shots the doctor gave him the pain was still there. Evelyn and I went over to his home one day. I sat down on the edge of his bed and I said, "Collins, where do you hurt?"

"Well," he said, "Rev [he always called me Rev], right here in my back."

I took his hand to shake it and he said, "Oh, don't shake my hand too roughly — I can feel it here in my back."

I knew he was really hurting. I said, "Collins, I'm going to pray for you."

He said, "Good."

I said, "Look at my hands a moment. My hands have no healing power but the hands of Jesus have healing power. When I touch you don't think about my hands. But just try to picture Christ coming into this house, coming into your bedroom. Collins, if Jesus Christ walked into your bedroom, right where you are on the bed today, what do you think would happen?"

He said, "He'd heal me."

"Well," I said, "Jesus said, 'I am with you always, even to the end of the world.' So just focus your faith on God, think now of our Lord coming in and putting His hands on you." I touched him and prayed and I could feel the Spirit of God. You know, when you're praying and making contact with God you can feel it. People say, "What do you feel?" I don't know how to explain it except you can feel it. I looked at him and said, "What's happening?"

Big tears rolled down his cheeks and he said, "Rev, I feel a warmth going into my back."

I said, "Do you think you can sit up on the side of the bed?"

He said, "I think so."

He sat up on the side of the bed and said, "Just give me your hand . . ."

I lifted him up, and when he stood to his feet his whole body rose free and strong. He was healed from his head to his feet by the power of faith in the living Christ.

You know, it seems so easy when you do it. It only seems hard when you don't do it. Once you get into the stream of faith and you're putting your mind upon Christ, you're seeing Him coming to you — it makes all the difference in the world. Just picture in your mind God coming to you in His Son Jesus Christ. Picture Jesus coming to you at the point of your need, whether you feel your sickness in the form of being down with financial obligations, or trouble in your marriage, or pain in your body, or fear in your mind, or problems in your home, or something else that has gone wrong. Picture Christ coming to you at the point of your need. Focus your faith on Him.

This came to me dramatically in our Jamaica Crusade in December 1968. Crowds of more than 50,000 people attended each service daily. The stadium was jampacked. I preached the first night on "The Centurion's Servant." This is the miracle told in Matthew 8:5-13, where the centurion came to Jesus and asked Him to pray for the healing of his servant and the centurion said to Jesus, "Speak the word only, and my servant shall be healed."

As I preached I felt I was on holy ground. I sensed great strength under the anointing of the Holy Spirit. That night I was checked by the Holy Spirit that I must not touch anybody with my hands lest they get their eyes completely on me and miss Jesus. When I finished preaching, I asked the team members and the Oral Roberts University students assisting me to kneel and touch each other. All eyes were focused on the platform. The power of God was present. The students knelt and prayed for one another, placing their hands on each other's shoulders. The crowd watched in obvious awe. The atmosphere was heavy with faith. Then I asked the team, the students, and the cooperating pastors to encircle the whole platform, facing the crowd, with one hand extended to the people and one hand raised to God. I asked each one in the crowd of 50,000 people to face his neighbor and touch him just as we had demonstrated on the platform. Then we prayed and many miracles happened.

Among them were two blind men. One man had gone blind when he was a young man. When someone in the great audience touched him, as we had instructed, he was healed. When he came up to the platform to testify, it was evident that he had been blind — his eyes were still milky. But by the time he left the platform they were almost completely clear. He could see as well as I could.

The other man had been blind from birth. He was dressed poorly. His hands were not the hands of a laborer; they were smooth and soft for he had never done any manual labor. When he came to the platform he stood close to me and kept saying, "It's different. Everything looks so different than I thought — the trees, the color — everything is different than I thought it would be. Everything is so wonderful!" And he continued to speak in astonishment and wonderment. It was a time of contact with God.

Another outstanding healing miracle was that of a woman who had been crippled for years. During the healing prayer this woman threw away her crutches and ran up to the platform to tell of her miracle. Someone followed her, trying to give her crutches back to her, and she said, "I don't need them."

I constantly urge people to get it out of their minds that God works magic. Get it out of your mind that some individual has personal healing power. At the best, we are only instruments. All healing is in God. He is our Source. Therefore, we must turn ourselves toward the Lord. He must become our Lord, the Source of our life.

A miracle is not something for nothing. It doesn't happen by our doing nothing. A miracle comes through faith. A miracle comes when we act upon our faith. When we DO something.

THE POINT OF CONTACT SETS THE TIME FOR YOUR HEALING

There was a couple in El Paso, Texas. The wife had been constantly ill, and in and out of bed for 8 years, and finally she was unable to even do her housework. So the husband had to work all day and then come home and do the housework. They were not church people. They hadn't even thought about God entering into their lives. There they were — just sort of cut off with their problems.

They had had the best that medicine had to offer but they still wound up with the same problem. Then they began watching our telecast and they began to think about God's power to heal. One day I preached about the point of contact and the husband caught on to the idea . . . SET THE TIME . . . SET THE TIME. He decided that at the close of the telecast when I prayed, that would be their time.

When the time came to pray I asked each one to touch someone in the room with them as a point of contact. This seemed strange to them. They had never touched each other in connection with prayer. But the more you turn yourself to God, the more you will turn to one another. Have you ever thought about that?

There they sat touching one another, trying to pray, and neither one of them was a Christian. But he later wrote me and said, "When you said, 'Now is the time! Release your faith and BE HEALED!' I felt a warmth start flowing through me. My wife looked at me and said, 'Honey, something happened to me,' I said to her, 'It's happening to me too.'

"Brother Roberts, today my wife is so much better. She is now able to do her own housework. She's not yet completely well but we believe she will be. We're both serving the Lord now and we're learning how to use our faith every day. THIS IS REAL. THIS IS REAL!!!"

Sometime ago Richard and I were on the Mike Douglas Show. As we came to the end of the interview Mike said, "I have one more question, Oral. I can understand your praying for people's healing face-to-face and their responding and receiving help. What I can *not* understand is how you do it on television. That camera there, I . . . "

I said, "Wait a minute, Mike. To me, that camera is a person. In fact, when I stand before that camera, I feel so close to the viewer that I feel like I can just reach out and touch him. And I think people feel that."

"How?" he said.

And I said, "By our closeness, by thinking about what Christ can do."

Recently I was speaking at a certain great church and a woman came up at the close of the service and said:

"Mr. Roberts, I must tell you this. My aged parents, in their 70's, have been very ill. My father is semiparalyzed and my mother has been ill also. They called me and I went to their home. As I came in, your telecast was on and they were sitting there before the TV screen. You were just coming to the end of your sermon and ready to pray. They motioned for me. I went over and knelt down between the two of them. I took my mother's hand and I took my father's hand, and as you stretched your hands out to pray I became their point of contact. As you prayed, we prayed. And something happened. My father was able to stand up. My mother said her pain was gone. I knew my father was healed because he went out to his automobile, got in, and drove it. He had not been able to drive. They decided to take a trip and they vacationed in New York City like a young couple. This happened in Salt Lake City to my parents."

Don't you see healing is not some big complicated thing? It's all in Christ. It's in our Lord. I cannot heal. If I could heal I'd heal everybody in the world right now. But somehow God has placed a miracle at the end of your faith. You will find God . . . the Source of all miracles . . . at the end of your faith.

Now let me summarize what I have been saying to you about the miracle of the point of contact:

1. **The point of contact is something you do, and when you do it you release your faith.** Your point of contact may be writing a letter to me . . . or laying your hands on my letter, or at the close of a radio or television program when I pray . . . or something else unrelated to me or my ministry. The point of contact is something YOU DO!

2. **The point of contact focuses your faith on God.** All healing is of the Lord. He is your Source. Therefore, you

must turn yourself toward the Lord. He must become your Lord. You must focus your faith on Him.

3. **The point of contact sets the time for your healing.** When you set a time for something to take place you reach a point of expectation. You begin to *expect* a miracle to happen. "Anytime faith" doesn't work but "expectant faith" sets the stage for a miracle.

The healing of Willie Phelps.

Here I am with Willie and he is telling me about his healing.

Willie, as he is today, holding one of his hunting trophies.

Mr. and Mrs. Phelps, today, looking at the photo of Willie that was carried on the cover of our magazine in 1950.

CHAPTER SIX

THE HEALING OF WILLIE PHELPS

(The simplest but greatest miracle of healing I ever saw)

IN TELLING YOU of the miracle received by Willie Phelps it takes me back to a minister from India approaching me between sessions at the World Conference on Evangelism in Berlin several years ago, and saying:

"Mr. Roberts, a mother brought her little sick child to me some time ago and asked me to pray that God would heal him. So I prayed for the little boy, only because she had asked me to, and he was healed. Nevertheless, I received some criticism because I prayed for his healing. Did I do right in praying for the little boy?"

I looked at the minister for a moment. This was not a "yes" or "no" question. And certainly we didn't have time for a long theological discussion on divine healing, etc. So as I looked at the minister I suddenly felt the presence of the Holy Spirit wash through me. And in a flash the Holy Spirit gave me a word of knowledge for him. "Why don't you ask the little boy?" I replied. He smiled, "Oh, yes, why don't I ask the little boy. I see what you mean, yes, yes."

I often think of that incident when I think about Willie Phelps who was healed in our Roanoke, Virginia Crusade in 1951. A few weeks ago we again contacted the Phelps family to inquire about Willie. We found that he works for a paint company in his city, lives at home with his parents, and is still — after 22 years — a living, breathing, walking testimony to a miracle. While we waited for Willie to come in from work, his mother told us what she recalls happening the night of Willie's miracle.

"As we stood in the semidarkness the snow began to fall. A chill swept through my body but the presence of God warmed my spirit. From all outward signs it looked hopeless, but I had a knowing deep down inside me that this was Willie's hour — God was going to heal him.

"We had already made two trips to Roanoke only to be turned away with the hundreds of other latecomers. This was our third try, over a hundred miles round trip — that was a long way, back in those days. When we arrived it was the same as before. The crowds were so thick that you could scarcely find the entrance. But it wouldn't have done any good. No one could get in. The auditorium was packed to overflowing. Tonight was Saturday night — the last night of the crusade—and I was feeling desperate.

"I looked over at Willie — I can see him like it was yesterday. He was standing there in the snow leaning on those little crutches and one shoe built up 2½ inches, his chubby little face full of expectancy, never doubting for one minute that this time we would get inside.

"I would have given up when they barred the doors, but when you're desperate you can't lose hope.

"As we stood shivering in the snow I silently prayed . . . and we walked. Pretty soon I heard someone say, 'They will be taking some ambulance cases into the invalid room pretty soon.' I didn't know what this meant but I thought this might be a chance for Willie to get in. So we pushed our way out of the crowd and around to the side, only to find another crowd. We waited there and prayed. Willie was the only one left in the crowd on crutches. Suddenly an usher stood in the door and said, 'The little boy on crutches – make way for him . . .' His daddy helped him through the crowd and they both went in. I was left outside. But I didn't care. Willie and his daddy were inside and I knew God could take care of the rest. Outside I praised the Lord in my heart, prayed . . . and waited. Pretty soon, the usher appeared at the door again and said:

"'The mother of the little crippled boy – let her in . . .' There was just room enough for the three of us to stand in the corner. As we listened to Brother Roberts' sermon over the loudspeaker my eyes swept across a roomful of suffering humanity – many seemingly more desperate than Willie. Yet, in spite of the stench of sickness and death, you could feel the atmosphere electric with hope.

"Then I looked at Willie leaning heavily on his crutches. His eyes sparkled and my mind went back 4 years before to the day he was injured. He had been as healthy and rowdy as any 6-year-old boy. But one day while playing and running through the house he accidentally fell on the andirons by the fireplace. I remember we didn't think much about it at the time. But in a few days he began to limp and complain about the pain in his hip. We took him to the doctor. He didn't find anything more than a bruise at the time and told us to bathe Willie three times a day, for an hour each time, in hot salt water.

"When this failed to bring relief we took Willie to the hospital. His leg had shrunk a full 2½ inches and he could not walk. The doctor at the hospital diagnosed his problem as Perthes' disease and said there was nothing that could be done for it . . . although they tried different means to relieve the pain.

"Willie was in the hospital for 3 weeks with a ten-pound weight attached to his leg. When this failed they placed him in a heavy cast up to his shoulders. This seemed to relieve the pain but when the cast was removed, one leg was still 2½ inches shorter than the other and Willie could not walk.

"The specialists devised a built-up shoe for him and fitted him with crutches. The first time I saw him trying to hobble around on that ugly shoe and those heavy crutches I thought my heart would break into a million pieces. The doctors tried to comfort me by saying, 'Mrs. Phelps, Willie is lucky to be able to walk, even with crutches . . . nine out of ten children with this disease *never* walk again . . .'

"So we had tried everything we knew and the doctors had done everything they knew, but Willie was a cripple. Now nothing less than a miracle would do.

"My thoughts were interrupted when suddenly the door opened and Brother Roberts came into the invalid room. The moment for which we had waited so long had finally arrived and, yet, it seemed ages before Brother Roberts finally got to us. By this time everyone in the room had been prayed for. Many had been instantly healed and some were still laughing and crying and praising God. For a moment it looked like Brother Roberts had missed Willie — he passed him by. My heart sank. I couldn't believe we had come this close, only to be overlooked. My heart broke. Tears soaked my face. I was lost in my own grief when suddenly I heard a voice weary with exhaustion, but full of compassion say:

" 'SON, WHAT ARE YOU DOING IN HERE?'

" 'I'm waiting for Oral Roberts.'

" 'What do you want with him?'

" 'I'm supposed to be healed tonight.'

" 'Son, I'm Oral Roberts.'

" 'You are?'

" 'Yes.'

" 'Well, I'm supposed to be healed tonight.'

"Then Brother Roberts looked down at Willie with a sort of tired smile and said, 'Do you believe that Jesus can heal you?'

"Willie said, 'Uh huh.'

"Then Brother Roberts touched Willie's head and said simply, 'BE HEALED IN THE NAME OF JESUS.' And he left the room, never turning back. BUT IN THAT INSTANT OUR MIRACLE HAPPENED.

"Brother Roberts didn't know until 18 months later when we returned to Roanoke for a second crusade. We brought Willie to tell about his miracle.

"Here's what happened:

"God's miracle power was working in that place that night. Willie was full of childlike faith. And when Brother Roberts prayed that simple prayer the divine healing power of God went through Willie's body. He was seemingly stunned for a moment. Then he yelled, 'MOM! I'M HEALED.' Quick as a wink he took off his shoe, threw his crutches aside, and said, 'I'M GOING TO WALK!' But he didn't walk . . . HE RAN! . . . and without the slightest limp. In an instant both legs became the same length. Willie had his miracle. And talk about a time! We had it — laughing and crying and hugging everybody and praising the Lord.

"This happened on a Saturday night and of course all the stores were closed the next day and we couldn't get Willie another pair of shoes until Monday. That was the longest Sunday I believe we ever spent. Willie kept begging me for new shoes and I kept saying, 'Honey, we'll get you some shoes tomorrow when the stores are open.'

"Finally Monday came — and we didn't need an alarm clock. Willie was up at the crack of dawn, raring to go.

"I can still see him. When the salesman slipped those normal shoes on Willie's feet he walked like a king. But the real excitement was yet to come. It was about 10 o'clock before we could get him to school.

"Willie says, 'When I walked into class that day the kids went wild. They had never seen me except on crutches. And now I was walking just like they did. When my teacher could quiet the class, she asked me to tell them what happened. I told them exactly how it all happened. As I talked, my teacher cried and the kids cheered and I was never so happy in my life.

" 'When I finished, my teacher said, "My! Willie, that must have cost a lot of money!" And I said, "No, teacher, it didn't cost one cent — Oral Roberts prayed and God healed me . . . it was a miracle." '

"From that time on, Willie has lived a normal, happy life. One of the things he had missed the most was deer hunting in the mountains with his daddy. But they made up for lost time and Willie has all kinds of trophies to show for his hunting skill. And I tell you, it takes a good pair of feet and legs to trudge up and down those mountain trails.

"God didn't move the mountains but He did something better—He gave Willie a miracle so he could climb over them."

☆　　☆　　☆

SOMETHING YOU SHOULD KNOW ABOUT PRAYER THAT LEADS TO MIRACLES...

Recently when I was in the Prayer Tower reading letters from the people and praying over their great needs, my heart just involuntarily cried out to God. I found myself praying real hard for the people. As I was there praying the Lord began to speak to my heart and to say:

DON'T PRAY HARD. PRAY EASY.

PRAYER DOESN'T DO IT. GOD DOES.

As I look back over this ministry and the outstanding miracles that have occurred, such as the healing of Willie Phelps, I realize that these miracles have not happened because of long, hard prayers. Often, it was a very short, simple prayer. You see, I pray for people the way the Holy Spirit directs me to pray for them because I am not the healer — GOD IS!

For example, I am seldom directed to use the laying-on-of-hands as I once was. Strangely, I am seeing more results through another point of contact the Holy Spirit impressed me to use for this present phase of my ministry which is:

TOUCH AND AGREE

Jesus said, "If two of you shall agree on earth as touching any [one] thing . . . it shall be done for them of my Father which is in heaven" (Matthew 18:19).

For years people focused on my hands and many were able to make them their point of contact. Then almost overnight the method was not nearly so effective. I have felt the presence of God in my hands from the beginning, and still do. I can't explain it. It's a mystery to me. But I feel it in my hands, particularly in my right hand.

When I returned to television with a new format in 1969, my guidance was to stretch forth my hands toward the people in need of healing BUT TO ASK THEM TO TOUCH ONE ANOTHER . . . to touch and agree!

Although I expected God to work through this new method (because He gave it to me), I am astounded sometimes at the miracle of it being so right for the now. Perhaps people have changed, perhaps there is a deep inner desire people feel to reach out and touch one another. I know I feel it. As we touch and agree, our Father will work His wonders.

Actually, you could very well say that's what happened with Willie Phelps. His mother's memory of it and mine are almost the same. The part I recall is finding him in the room and thinking he was alone. At least I only remember him, not his parents.

I told Willie I was so tired I didn't feel I could pray, but I would touch him and sort of breathe a prayer IF AT THE SAME TIME HE WOULD TRY TO BELIEVE. He nodded his head. My touch was very brief . . . but what was happening was we were TOUCHING AND AGREEING. God did the healing.

What I am seeing today is *touching* and *agreeing* at a distance. When a person writes me, and I write back, we join in faith and *touch* and *agree!* The same as I reach forth my hands on TV or radio and people touch in their homes — TOUCHING AND AGREEING — it is God doing the healing.

You will be hearing more and more from me on TOUCH AND AGREE . . .

Our family on a television program. Left to right: Richard, Roberta, me, Evelyn, Rebecca, and Ron.

CHAPTER SEVEN

MIRACLES IN THE LIVES OF MY FOUR CHILDREN

(Their tribulations, trials, and triumphs as the children of a man who is in the ministry of healing)

I HAVE NEVER BEEN ASHAMED of the healing ministry of our Lord Jesus Christ. I've had many successes and I've had many failures. When I began I made up my mind that I would obey God and pray for people — whether they were healed or not healed. Only God can heal . . . I cannot. I would pray and believe and leave the results with God. I have prayed for some people and wonderful miracles have occurred. I have prayed for others and nothing happened. When this happens you have to die to what other people are going to say. You have to put it out of your mind and just go on doing what God has called you to do and thank Him for what He is doing.

For years I underwent terrible things. I was called every name imaginable. But I knew what I had was real. I knew I had something in my soul. I knew that people were getting help . . . they were learning how to reach out to God and receiving miracles in their lives. And this kept me going.

But it wasn't always easy for our four children . . . especially during the early years of this ministry when prayer for the sick was so new and misunderstood . . . when the charismatic move of the Holy Spirit was just beginning to be experienced in our churches.

All of our children have known Christ as Savior from a very early age and all of them believe that God still performs miracles.

I remember when Ronnie, our older son, was just a little boy. My mother was spending the night with us and she had a terrible cough. She kept coughing throughout the night. Finally, Ronnie put his hand on her and prayed. Then he said, "Grandmother, you won't cough anymore." And she didn't.

Ronnie finished high school as a top student and one of the big universities accepted him. (This was before ORU opened.) How proud Evelyn and I were. But after he had been there a few weeks, he called us. He was deeply distressed. The professors had been tampering with his faith. They seemed to feel that if they could shake the faith of Oral Roberts' son they would be doing something great.

I went to his side immediately. He began to fire questions at me that the professors had put to him. "What about it, Dad? Can you answer them?" he said.

I said, "Some of them, yes; others, no."

He said, "Well, where does that leave you?"

I said, "JUST EXACTLY WHERE YOU FOUND ME, RON, WITH FAITH IN GOD. Faith is for what you don't understand, Son. You nor your professors nor anyone else can understand everything about God by reason alone. For example, I could ask, Where were you when God made the world? Where were your professors when God created the earth out of nothing?"

Then we sat down and went back to the Bible and to the basics of our faith. "Ron," I said, "Have you ever felt the presence of God?"

He said, "Sure, Dad, many times."

"Well, then explain it."

"I can't, Dad."

I said, "It's like trying to explain how a black cow that eats green grass gives white milk that makes yellow butter, isn't it."

Ron said, "I can't explain it."

"And I've never found a Ph.D. in any college who can explain it. You can drink the milk and eat the butter but you can't explain it."

Slowly Ron began to understand that while there are many things we grasp with our intellect, there are spiritual realities that can be comprehended only by faith. We had prayer together and felt the presence of God. When I left to return home, I felt that Ronnie had been strengthened within to face the battle of retaining his faith in the classroom.

Each of our four children have had their own individual struggles and their own experiences in believing God for miracles. Sometime ago they appeared on one of our half-hour television programs and shared some of these experiences. I think they tell it best in their own words so I'm including here the transcript of that interview. They told the TRUTH — even when it hurt — but they told it like it was and like it is. I know you will enjoy sharing a bit of our family secrets with us.

ORAL ROBERTS' FAMILY DIALOGUE AS PRESENTED ON TV

Oral: Well, I'm so proud to present the members of my family. On my left is my oldest son Ron, and here's my oldest daughter Rebecca. Hi, Rebecca.

Rebecca: Hi, Dad!

Oral: And here on my right is my youngest daughter Roberta, and you all know who this young gentleman is — Richard. And this is Evelyn my wife. Honey, on Christmas Day, 1938, when we started out together in our marriage, I don't think we dreamed that we'd have four wonderful children like these.

Evelyn: Right. When we see them all on the program now, the girls are so beautiful and the boys are so handsome. Dear me, what does that make us?

Oral: Well, Honey, what could you expect?

Evelyn: But really, though, you are very young and handsome to have such beautiful children.

Oral: Darling, flattery will get you everywhere. Well, Ron is in the University of Southern California, working on a Ph.D. in linguistics. [Ron has now finished the classwork on his Ph.D. and is teaching in Tulsa while he is writing his thesis.] We're thrilled to have him, his wife Carol, and little Rachel so close to home again.

Ron: Right.

Oral: And Rebecca is a young housewife, and I like to think a community leader in Tulsa. Roberta married Ron Potts, also an ORU student, a year and a half ago. [Roberta and Ron both graduated from ORU last spring and are now working with us in the ministry.] And this is Richard, my younger son, who is working with me on the television program and in the ministry.

Richard: Thank you, I appreciate that.

Oral: Evelyn, it hasn't always been easy, has it?

Evelyn: No. Because we had to travel so much that sometimes I think perhaps the children, as all normal children would, resented having us away so much. You remember the time that Richard resented our being gone and chopped the end of his bed off? Do you remember that?

Oral: Just the bed post.

Richard: Yes — just the post, not the whole thing.

Oral: Yes, I remember quite well. Ron, as you grew up and your father was traveling over America and the world, and you were going to school, what are some of the things you faced — the struggles?

Ron: Well, Dad, kids aren't very tactful, and every now and then someone would come up to me and say very bluntly, "Is your father a fake?" I don't know what they expected me to say when they asked silly questions like that. Of course there were many advantages too. I got to travel a great deal and I had the experience of living in the home that you lived in, Dad.

Oral: Rebecca, were there any times it was hard to be my daughter? I'm asking this, so just go ahead and say it if it's true.

Rebecca: Well, yes, it was, Dad, especially at times. In a way I really never have been anyone in my own right. You see, I was first your daughter, and then I was married and I became my husband's wife, and then when my children were born I became their mother . . .

Oral: Yes.

Rebecca: And now I'm Richard's sister. (*laughter*) I can't ever seem to be anyone in my own right. Oh, I really am. I'm just kidding. When you develop confidence and you feel a worth in yourself, finally, then the feelings that you had as a child don't bother you anymore. I don't mind being your daughter; I am really proud to be your daughter. Very proud.

Oral: Thank you. I'm grateful to have you as my daughter. Richard, how about yourself as you grew up?

Richard: Well, I went through the normal trials. I can remember many times, especially when I was much younger — around the age of 10 — wondering why you were gone so much and why many times you had to have mother with you. You left us with baby sitters and somehow that just wasn't enough. It was very difficult. I can remember sometimes your being gone as much as 3 weeks out of one month. And that was tough.

Oral: And I might be in Africa or Asia or . . .

Richard: That's right.

Oral: South America . . .

Richard: That's right. We would live from day to day wondering whether we were going to get a phone call from you, especially when you were overseas. Sometimes we didn't get to hear from you for a week and sometimes we'd go 2 weeks without hearing from you.

Ron: Richard, if I may interrupt, I'd like to say that we were in many ways very lucky to have some very lovely people who stayed with us while Mother and Dad were gone.

Richard: That's true, of course.

Ron: We were very fortunate to find people who were good to us.

Oral: How about you, Roberta? Give us some of your feelings.

Roberta: Well, it seems like I must have been different from the rest. I don't believe I missed having my parents gone. I suppose I didn't realize they were supposed to be there.

Oral: Oh! That really hurt.

Roberta: Well, Dad, you told us to tell the truth.

Oral: I did! Go ahead! Give it to us straight.

Roberta: To me, you were someone that came home every once in a while and I didn't really know why. Then you left again.

Oral: In other words — Mother, who's that stranger?

Roberta: No, not really, but I did wonder why. I guess you don't miss anything you've never had very much of.

Oral: Of course, you were the least.

Roberta: I was the youngest.

Oral: You're 5'-8" tall now, and you're the youngest, but not the shortest. Ron, what do you think might have been the most difficult experience of your life? I know that you were in Stanford University and then you went into the army. I recall one episode when your mother and I came to see you, and you were flat on your back.

Ron: Well, yes. Shortly after going through basic training in the army, I was assigned to the Defense Language Institute in Monterey, California. I came down with infectious hepatitis. By the time I realized that I had it, and by the time the army doctors were convinced I had it, I was quite ill. They put me in the hospital and called you and Mother immediately and said that you'd better come out. The doctor there was very good. He said that it would take 4 months for me to recover. But you and Mother came and you prayed for me, and a month later I was up and out of bed.

Oral: You know, the thing that stands out in our minds the most, that you and I have talked the most about, Evelyn . . .

Evelyn: About his healing, you mean?

Oral: Yes.

Evelyn: Oh, yes! When the doctor said it would be 4 months and we went in there and said, "Ronnie, it can be 4 months, but when God gets on the case it doesn't have to be 4 months." We just simply rebuked the devil and told him to take his hands off God's property because we had given Ronnie to the Lord when he was little.

Oral: All the children, we gave to God.

Evelyn: All of them. When we prayed this way and our faith was positive — really positive — it helped Ronnie's faith to become positive. Then, really, he was healed. He was dismissed from that hospital after what? Three weeks, Ronnie?

Ron: Four weeks.

Oral: Four weeks. Shortened it from 4 months to 1 month. That meant something to us to see that miracle.

Rebecca, what spiritual experience, or moment of truth, or something you have passed through, as you've had faith in God, can you tell us about, or what have the concepts of this ministry done in your life? I know I'm rambling in this question but I'm trying to drive at something that is an epic in your own experience.

Rebecca: Well, when you have children this brings something home to you. Things your parents tell you really don't mean much to you until you have children of your own and you realize you have the responsibility for directing their lives. Then what you say, and what you do as an example, can really mean something, it can make the difference between success and failure in many ways . . .

Oral: Are you saying that as you were growing up and we were saying these things to you, that they didn't mean much until you were married and had three little children of your own?

Rebecca: That's an old cliché. I know you told me as I was growing up, "Now, this won't mean much to you now, but when you get children of your own . . ." and I thought, oh, boy! But it did, I must say. It did. Now my children are 10 and 5, and a little boy 2 years old, and I want them to contribute to the world. I want them to be a positive force. I think that has meant more to me than anything. The things you have taught us in our lifetime — thinking positively, looking at the world through positive eyes. It makes a difference in everything I do. Things seem different to me and if they seem different to me, then I come across in a different way — to my children and to anyone else.

Oral: Would you agree that the concepts had some other impact upon you, Roberta?

Roberta: Yes, they really did. I'd like to say one thing about healing. I guess when I was little, I didn't know enough not to believe that God heals. I remember once we were in Pittsburgh and I had gotten really sick. I was so sick, and you know when you get sick you think the whole world is coming apart. You were in the other room, Dad, talking to someone on the phone and evidently you were praying for them. Well, I just took this as if it were for me. I sat there and got healed myself. You didn't even know you were praying for me, but I took it and I was praying at the same time. This has happened so many times. And when you come on TV, if there's anything wrong with me I use that as if it were directed toward me.

Oral: It's still meaningful to you then?

Roberta: Oh, yes, very much so.

Oral: How about you, Richard?

Richard: Yes, it's very meaningful to me. In relation to what Roberta was just saying, you can use it as a point of contact; it's something you can mentally grasp hold of. I was thinking of an incident of healing that I had in my life. I remember—if you'll recall—at one time I had 22 warts . . .

Oral: Yeah, I remember . . .

Richard: On my left hand. My mother came in and very triumphantly said, "You're going to the doctor and you're going to have those burned off." I was about 10 or 12 and that scared me half to death. You came home and I told you about it, and I remember you said, "Evelyn, you leave that boy alone; he and I and the Lord are going to take care of those warts." We went off into another room and we had a very quiet simple prayer. I didn't know how God would do it, but I just believed that when you prayed they'd go away, and inside of 2 weeks every wart was gone. I think the Bible talks about having faith like a child or having childlike faith.

Oral: Let me see that hand.

Richard: Not a wart on it.

Evelyn: I was thinking of what someone at school said to Roberta one day.

Oral: Was that ORU?

Evelyn: No, when she was in high school! You want to tell about it, Roberta?

Roberta: A girl said to me, "Roberta, can your dad heal?" And I said, "No, can yours?" Her face got all red.

Oral: You were saying to her that Someone could heal, it just wasn't an individual.

Roberta: Right.

Evelyn: I know all of the children have been helped through the Seed-Faith concept, but as a student at ORU, I believe Roberta might have something she wants to say about it . . .

Oral: About giving?

Roberta: Yes, Dad. I've learned so much from this giving principle. You know I've been shy all my life and I was always withdrawn and didn't want to know other people. As I get older and I read my Bible more, I've learned that you must give to other people. And as I do it, I enjoy it. It's so hard for me to be able to talk to people and be what I am without putting on a front, but when I do, that is giving to them.

Oral: Yes, it certainly is.

Roberta: And God gives back to me and it's beautiful.

Oral: Well, children, we're thankful for what God has done for our family. We've been through some deep waters and trials and tribulations, and every now and then something strikes one of us and it hurts, and we know what it means to hurt. As Roberta said when she was sick, "the world falls apart." But God has been with us and we've experienced miracle after miracle.

Johnny Cash and I when he appeared on one of our CONTACT Specials.

CHAPTER EIGHT

THE MIRACLE OF
OUR TELEVISION MINISTRY

THERE'S A SPIRITUAL EXCITEMENT about our television programs. I can scarcely wait to get to that camera, for when I'm talking into that television camera I'm talking to just one person. I feel an extreme closeness to the individual person and his need. There's no traveling or waiting — the person watching and I can come together there in the quietness of his own home. I can share God's Word; I can reach forth my hands and pray for him ACCORDING TO HIS NEED. I can *touch and agree* with him through the Spirit. We can become one in faith and love. This has become the most effective means God has given me to help people find God and get their needs met. Our being there on TV each week and each quarter in hour-long, prime-time Specials is one of the continuing miracles of this ministry.

In 1954, when we first went on television, key men in the industry said it couldn't be done. They said we couldn't film in the big tent. They said we couldn't get stations to run our programs. But we did! For the first time multitudes — right in their own living rooms—saw God's healing power. Many used the prayer time during the telecast as a point of contact for the releasing of their faith to find healing and wholeness through Jesus Christ.

When we began our ministry on nationwide television the name *Oral Roberts* was still new to people. But down in Wichita Falls, Texas, there was a soldier with his wife Anna. She'd had polio for several years and was confined to a wheelchair. Their name was Williams. One Sunday while our telecast was on I was praying for the people and she said to her husband, "Pick me up . . . I'm going to walk."

They had been listening to our telecasts for some time. They were Baptist people who had great faith. When he lifted her, at first her feet just went out from under her. She had no strength. But she insisted, "Let my feet touch the floor," and when they did the Spirit of God came upon her and her legs straightened, her ankle bones received strength, and she stood. Then she walked. And she said, "Give me my baby" (whom she had never been able to lift). She took him and just whirled him around saying, "I'm healed; I'm healed."

Well, the news of her healing spread and the next morning it was in the headlines. I picked up a newspaper in a large city and there it was: MIRACLE SAVES POLIO VICTIM. They didn't mention my name but the whole nation knew whose telecast it was.

Paul Harvey, the noted news commentator, flew down to Wichita Falls, Texas, to interview Anna Williams in a public auditorium that was packed. The pastor of her church was there. The great crowd was there. And Paul Harvey said, "Ladies and Gentlemen, Mrs. Anna Williams . . ." and she came WALKING down the aisle. This was the beginning of a new surge . . . a new understanding of God's healing love in our nation.

This was not an isolated miracle but it was perhaps the most publicized. Our mail regularly told of other miracles that happened as a result of our weekly telecasts.

Then in the spring of 1967 — after 13 years of nation-wide television — the Lord let me see that that phase of our television ministry was ended . . . that I should — at least for a time — devote my time to answering my mail, to the University, and other aspects of this ministry. At the time, I felt that we would someday go back on TV but I wanted it to be the Lord's time and hour.

During the 2 years that we were off TV I was restless. I knew that I had obeyed God, yet inside I was troubled. I saw our nation forsaking God. I saw an increasing number of young people becoming confused as they saw adults turning everywhere for help except to God. I heard people who went to church cry, "Where is the God who is relevant to my needs . . . NOW???" I was reaching out for a way to reach these masses. I knew that television could be a part of the answer but I also knew that our method would have to be different than it had been before. The previous 20 years God had said, *Go into all the world and preach the gospel to every creature* . . . Now as I struggled with this great need, deep inside I heard God say:

"GO INTO EVERY MAN'S WORLD"

He was telling me that in order to go into all the world and preach the gospel to everyone, I must do it by going into every man's world. Well, I didn't know how so I said, "How, God?"

In my heart God spoke:

"Do it through weekly and quarterly television programs."

As I continued to seek God He began to unfold to me how we could have such programs. He led me to a godly producer and to a Christian who was a great music arranger and orchestra leader, who helped us in designing the format and music that would speak to the hearts of people — where they are now — in the midst of the 20th-century problems and crises. An excitement began to build within me. By faith I saw God meeting the needs of millions of people . . .

right where it's at . . .
in their homes . . .
through the medium of television.

On the other hand . . .

I thought of the continuous struggle we would have with television stations to sell us time.

I thought of the tremendous cost . . . (Oral Roberts University was still young and the financial load was — and is — unbelievable).

I thought of the possibility of failure . . . of those of my partners who might not understand our new approach . . . and of my need to communicate clearly with them.

I thought of the physical drain on myself and the students to produce these programs week . . . after week . . . after week.

There have been many times when I have been really scared to "seed for a miracle" and this was one of them. IT WAS A RISK OF FAITH — A BIG RISK! At least that's the way it felt to me. I really had mixed feelings. I was excited . . . and I was also shaking inside!

Well, we made the announcement to the staff that we planned to return to nationwide TV on an entirely new format, geared to meet the needs of the people NOW. Evelyn and I were looking to God and we decided together to *seed for our miracle* and to expect a return in the form of our need. And our immediate need was financing for the pilot TV program.

Shortly after this a young minister came to us, wanting to buy a piece of equipment that we no longer needed. It was an expensive piece of equipment. My immediate reaction was:

HERE'S THE MONEY WE NEED TO MAKE
OUR PILOT TELEVISION PROGRAM!!!

But again, deep inside I heard God say:

"NO, ORAL, I WANT YOU TO *GIVE* IT TO HIM."

It didn't make sense to GIVE this equipment away when we needed money so desperately. I knew what my men would think about it. I could almost hear them saying, "GIVE IT AWAY???" So I argued with the Lord a bit.

"Lord, my men will have to agree because the equipment belongs to the Association."

Then the Lord seemed to say, *How about the Association doing a little seeding for a miracle?*

When I presented it to the men they agreed. It was seed we sowed. AND IT COST US SOMETHING. It was given out of our want, our need. We saw that until there is some sacrifice, you have not truly given. You've merely given out of your surplus. We determined to . . .

GIVE GOD OUR BEST, THEN ASK HIM FOR HIS BEST . . . THE GREATER THE SACRIFICE, THE GREATER THE BLESSING

"For with the same measure that ye mete [GIVE] withal it shall be measured [GIVEN] to you again" (Luke 6:38).

Well, thank God, He took that piece of equipment we gave as a seed we sowed and multiplied it over and over again in supplying finances for our first taping, ON PRIME TV TIME, and the many other expenses involved in our television ministry. The harvest from that first seed-sowing is history now. But we are continuing to give as seed we

sow and to look to God as the Source of our total supply.
And we are expecting the miracles that we MUST have
every day in order to *remain* on TV.

March 1969 we returned to TV with our first quarterly
hour-long Special on prime TV time across America. Richard
and Patti and the World Action Singers and guest star, the
late Mahalia Jackson, joined me in reaching out to millions
of lives through that telecast.

Our mail response broke all-time records. People wrote
to tell us how God was working in their lives. People from
all walks of life:

people who had never written us before . . .
people from every church background . . .
and people from no church at all.

In their letters they shared their victories, their burdens, and
asked for special prayer.

It was a miracle that we were back on television (especially at a time when station owners were reluctant and
often flatly refused to sell time to religious broadcasters)
but NO MIRACLE STANDS ALONE. For wrapped up in
each great miracle are often several others that people don't
know about.

One of the great miracles of that first quarterly prime-
time Special was that my son Richard appeared as a soloist.
You see, there was a time when Richard refused to sing
for me . . .

A MIRACLE OF RECONCILIATION

As Richard grew up, a gap grew between us. He began
to sing for coffeehouses and to lean toward show business.
The more I wanted him to sing for the Lord and me, the
less he wanted to.

One Sunday morning I asked him to sing for me at a seminar at ORU and he said, "No, Dad, I don't want to sing for you."

It shouldn't have hurt me, but it did. It really got down inside.

Later Richard attended a state university. He was doing his own thing. And I was praying and wondering about his gifted voice which was being developed more fully all the time.

Then one day he came home. He said, "Dad, let's go out and play a game of golf." We went out on the golf course and he was hitting the ball a mile. He is a tremendous golfer. I am a pretty good golfer myself once in a while but I couldn't hit the ball that day because I was all bound up inside. My mind was not on the game. As I would talk to Richard I could see he was turning me off. And I said, "OK, let's just go."

So we picked up our clubs right in the midst of the game and went to the car. We sat there and just glared at each other. And I will remember it as long as I live. He said:

"Dad, get off my back!"

Then it came to me that maybe I was on his back — maybe I was trying to save him. I was not letting God do it. I thought about it a moment. I calmed down and I began to silently pray. (Frankly, I didn't know WHAT to say to God.)

I said, "OK, Richard, give me your hand." With his hand in mine I said, "From this moment I am off your back. I am going to put you in the hands of God."

I felt then it was God's battle and not mine.

Richard went back to the state university. Then one day his mother received a phone call and Richard said,

"Mom, do you suppose that Oral Roberts University would accept me for next year?"

She asked me and I said, "I don't know. Richard has taken up a habit or two." When he came to me I told him he couldn't do the things he was doing and be a student on our campus.

He said, "I can quit doing those things."

I said, "That will be up to you."

There is a point in dealing with your children when it has to be at arm's length. You are no longer emotionally involved. They are released to God and you can act without fear. The Holy Spirit operating in your life takes the gift of faith and drops it into your heart so that you can look upon your problems from the vantage point of God himself and believe as God believes.

Richard enrolled at ORU and he followed the rules of the campus. But we were still having problems. Then he fell in love with Patti, the girl who is now his wife.

Shortly before their wedding date something happened to their line of communication, particularly in spiritual matters. Although Patti was very much in love with Richard, she knew they didn't have a chance if they got bogged down there. She told him, "Richard, between Christians, and especially between Christians who love each other, there is a communication. You are of one mind and your utmost goal is to serve the Lord and to live the way He wants you to live. I feel that somehow we are missing each other on this. It frightens me because I know that marriage is for life. Richard, I know you are a Christian, but of what earthly good are you to God? If you die you will go to heaven, but what are you worth to God now?"

She later told me, "I was searching for an inner commitment in Richard that said, 'Lord, if You call me to the wilds of Africa or to Brazil or wherever, I will go because I love You.'"

At the time, Evelyn happened to be with me in California. She said, "Oral, I feel impressed to go home." When she has these feelings I never oppose her. She got on a plane and was home within a few hours.

Richard was living in the dorm on campus at the time. His mother hadn't been home but a short time when he walked into the house. He said, "Mother, I'm so glad you are home. I've got to talk to you."

Evelyn said, "What is the trouble, Richard?"

"Well, something has happened to Patti. She can't seem to understand that I love her, and I really do."

Then he said, "Mother, she is going to call the wedding off."

Evelyn said, "Well, Richard, when you committed your life to the Lord recently, did you say, 'Lord, I will live for You if You will give me Patti'? You can't compromise with God. God wants all of you or nothing. Now He may or may not give you Patti. You can live without Patti but you can't live without the Lord. The Lord wants all of you, without reservations."

Then he got down on his knees and put his head in his mother's lap like he used to when he was a little boy, and they really prayed. And something happened inside Richard. He looked up, smiling through his tears, and he said, "It is all right, Mother. It is all right. I don't want to give up Patti but if that is the way the Lord wants it, I must serve God, regardless."

Then he picked up the phone and called me in California. He said, "Dad, everything is OK now."

I knew what he meant. *Dad, you are not on my back anymore.*

The next morning Richard saw Patti and he told her what had happened. But he didn't have to tell her. She said, "I was praying last night too. And suddenly my burden lifted. I knew something had happened. I didn't know what, exactly, but I wasn't worried anymore. Richard, I am ready to marry you."

They were married in November 1968. It has been a joy to Evelyn and me to see them putting God first in their total lives — their home, their time, their giving, and especially their talents. Richard is deeply involved in God's work with me. He and Patti are touching the hearts of thousands with their consecrated singing talents as they minister with us on our television programs.

You know, it's great to have a son stand before the TV cameras and minister through song, under God's anointing, to millions of people. It's also great to have a son behind the scenes who knows how to pray when the going gets rough. Richard says now, "Dad, you're not on my back any longer but I'm at your side."

I remember when we made our Special at Expo '70 in Japan. We faced all kinds of problems. The language barrier almost finished us before we started. It was extremely warm and some of the World Action Singers began to pass out from the heat. It just seemed that the devil worked overtime to prevent the taping of that Special. Right in the middle of everything the camera crew went on strike one night at midnight.

That particular night Evelyn and I had such a burden to pray for our producer. At the time, we did not know about the strike. But we could feel the hand of Satan pushing against us. As we were praying Richard and Patti came in and joined us. Finally Richard laid hands on each of us and commanded Satan — in the name of Jesus — to take his hands off God's property. The presence of the Lord filled the room and we cried and rejoiced as we felt new strength pouring into us.

God answered our prayer that night, for the next day our producer was able to get a new crew together at the last moment. Once again, a miracle pulled us out of the fire.

THE MIRACLE OF OUR GUEST STARS

I believe another of the great miracles of our television ministry has been the guest stars that God has sent to us. Their names and talents have drawn millions of viewers to our telecasts that we might not otherwise have been able to minister to. Their personal testimonies have blessed millions. Among them have been Dale Evans, Andrae Crouch, Pat and Shirley Boone, Pearl Bailey, Burl Ives, Della Reese, the Lennon Sisters, Johnny Cash, Anita Bryant, Tennessee Ernie Ford, Billy Graham, and many others.

I was deeply moved by Johnny Cash's testimony on one of our Contact Specials. He is among the first of our guest stars to give a personal witness of the Holy Spirit experience in his life. And I want to share that interview with you here.

THE JOHNNY CASH INTERVIEW

Oral Roberts: Johnny Cash knows the low and the high road of struggle. He knows what it is to pull an old cotton sack down between the cotton rows in the South. He knows what it is to walk on the dark side of life, to have his back to the wall. He knows what struggle is. All through those years he wrote those great meaningful songs about his struggles and about the problems and struggles of other people — songs that we relate to, songs that touch the heart. I'm so proud of this man and I'm proud of my friendship with him. He is now at the top of his music career as a superstar, but above all he is a wonderful, warm, loving human being . . . Johnny, the Lord has given you so much.

Johnny Cash: Well, you know, you never really start living until you start giving something back to Him. That's what I've found.

Oral: That's right and we can see the great change in your life. It was real news across America when Johnny Cash found our Lord Jesus Christ.

Johnny: Well, I'm trying harder as the days go by. You know, I knew He was there all along. I just took a while in turning to Him.

Oral: About a year and a half ago you and your lovely wife June received the baptism with the Holy Spirit — the charismatic experience. It's wonderful, isn't it?

Johnny: Yes, it is . . .

Oral: And this move of the Holy Spirit across the world is really something right now, isn't it?

Johnny: Yes, you can feel it moving all across this great land. There are strange and great things happening.

Oral: Johnny, in just a few moments we are going to show a film clip on this Contact Special of the great film that you narrated there in Israel, called "Gospel Road." But before you tell about it, I want you to know that my wife Evelyn and several of us have already viewed this film. And in my opinion it is the greatest film of our Lord's life that I have ever seen. As you sang some of the songs you wrote and the songs of Kris Kristofferson and others . . . the crucifixion . . . Mary Magdalene, played by your wife June — I tell you, we were in tears. It was the most deeply I've been moved in years.

Johnny: Bless your heart.

Oral: Now, will you give us a little background on the film clip, which will be the first time it will have been seen on national television.

Johnny: Well, I'd like to say this — not only are prayers answered, but dreams come true.

Oral: Yes.

Johnny: I know it's in the Bible somewhere — you'd know where it is — about dreams and visions and the young will prophesy.

Oral: Second chapter of the books of Acts, the Holy Spirit chapter, "Your young men shall see visions, and your old men shall dream dreams."

Johnny: That's it. I knew it was there somewhere. It started 6 years ago in Israel when June and I went the first time — the first day we were there. We woke up that morning and she said to me, "Last night I dreamed I saw you on a mountaintop in Israel. You had a Bible in your hand and you were talking about Jesus." At that time I didn't want to talk about that. But we went on up the country and passed Tiberias on the northern shore of Galilee. There's a beautiful mountain named Mt. Arbel, and when she saw that mountain she said, "That's it, that's were I dreamed I saw you last night."

Well, we talked about that from time to time, about going back some day and doing our story of Jesus . . . walking where He walked, telling His story the way we honestly felt it and saw it ourselves. And we hoped that other people would see it with believability and that they might be entertained as well as spiritually uplifted.

You know, once in every man's life there comes a time when he has to do that one thing that says to the world, "This is my contribution. This is what my life has to say. This is what I was put on this earth for." So that's what

"Gospel Road" is for June and me — our dream come true — our contribution.

Oral: It's being released now, isn't it, across the nation?

Johnny: We're very proud to say that we've made arrangements with 20th Century Fox to distribute our film now worldwide.

Oral: That's a miracle within itself, isn't it?

Johnny: It really is.

At this point, Johnny narrates a portion of his film with the actual background music and effects. To me, this short 3 minutes of the Special is one of the most moving segments of the program, and I know you'll be deeply moved by it.

Johnny's appearance on our Special ended with a roar of applause from the audience and a promise from him that he would return to ORU for a future chapel service. The response to this, needless to say, was almost deafening.

As I stand before the people week after week through television, it's a far cry from the first audience of slightly more than 1,000 who heard me in 1947 and received my ministry of God's Word and my prayers.

According to the American Research Bureau, our Sunday morning telecasts are rated No. 1 among the syndicated religious programs. This means there are millions of people in front-row seats, right in their living rooms across America, Canada, and other countries, viewing our telecasts each Sunday morning — and our quarterly CONTACT Specials. This past Christmas our rating was 48,000,000 viewers in the United States alone! There were another 5 million in Canada. But to me, it wasn't those millions, it was just one person with a need and I was reaching out to touch him with the power of my Savior Jesus Christ.

Yes, God is moving across the earth today in a way never before conceived by mankind. And people are being touched to the very core of their being, lives being transformed and saved, bodies being healed, broken homes mended, drug and alcohol addicts being restored, financial needs being met. And as we continue to teach and preach, to touch and agree, and pray for the needs of humanity through this phenomenal media of TV, the people are writing us and sharing with us how they are learning through this ministry to move into the miracle realm.

Remember, God is the Master over demons.

CHAPTER NINE

THE MIRACLE OF
EXORCISM

NOW I WANT TO SHARE with you some actual cases of demon-possessed people and how God used me as His instrument of "exorcism," or to cast out the demon.

In the early '60s I was in a crusade in the municipal auditorium at Raleigh, North Carolina. At the close of the message I gave an invitation to men and women there to come forward and accept Christ as their personal Savior. Then I began my prayers for the healing of people . . . that is, the healing of their body or the healing of their mind or the healing of some problem or need in their life. In our crusades we always had what we called a healing line. Hundreds of people would line up and come by and we would pray for the healing of these individuals.

On this particular occasion I was asked by a family to go outside and pray for their daughter who was in an automobile, because she was not in condition to be brought inside the building. She was considered dangerous to the point of harming other people. Knowing that the girl was probably demon-possessed, I asked a friend of mine, Mr. John Wellons, to go with me. (I've always made it a rule, if possible, never to pray for a demon-possessed person when I'm alone. I always try to have somebody with me. I recommend that to any other Christian or minister who is called upon to pray for a demon-possessed person. Remember that when our Lord sent His followers out, He sent them *two by two* (Luke 10:1). And they returned with great joy saying that even the devils were subject to them in the name of Jesus. They went out *two by two.*)

So John and I made our way through the automobiles in the parking lot to this particular car. As we came near we heard a voice. And this voice spoke in a very distinct, loud way, and said:

"He is approaching from behind the automobile." We took a few more steps and this voice said:

"It's Oral Roberts."

Then the voice said:

"He's coming on the left side of the automobile . . . " By this time I didn't know whether my friend was going to go on with me or not. I put my hand on him and I said, "Just hold it," because I had been through this type of thing before.

You remember in the Bible that when the demons in people encountered Jesus Christ they always knew who He was. Sometimes they would say, "Jesus . . . I know thee who thou art, the Holy One of God" (Mark 1:24).

THE SEVEN SONS OF SCEVA

In Acts 19 there is the record of seven sons of Sceva, a Jew, who had observed the ministry of St. Paul and had seen him exorcizing demons through the name of Jesus, so they undertook a ministry of casting out devils. But they were not followers of Jesus Christ. They had no idea what exorcism really is. They came to a certain individual who was possessed with devils and they said, "We adjure you by

Jesus whom Paul preacheth [that you come out of this man]."
They recognized the man had demons and they were calling
the demons out by the Christ that Paul knew; not the one
they knew, but the one that Paul knew. The demons used
the man's voice and said, "Jesus I know, and Paul I know;
but who are ye?" (Acts 19:15).

Then the man whom the demons possessed, leaped upon
these seven men and tore their clothes off (Acts 19:16).
(The last we heard of them, they were still running.)

Those of us who have been in this ministry long enough
to have dealt with a large number of people know how
knowledgeable demons are.

Well, as we approached the car the demon, using the
girl's voice, said, "Now whatever you do, don't let him put
his right hand on you."

When I came to the left side of the car she was in the
front seat on the right side. I put my head in the open win-
dow and she began to cower and to draw herself over
against the other side of the automobile. Her head was
down. Her eyes were shut. Her hands were over her eyes.
She had not physically seen me. There was no effort to
operate on a sense level of sight, feeling, hearing, tasting
and smelling — the sense level upon which we all live. Here
was a woman whose eyes were completely covered, whose
head was down, and yet was able to see me coming. She
knew my name. She was able to discern what I was there to
do. This demon was telling her, "Whatever you do, don't
let him touch you with his right hand."

When I reached my hand in, this demon said, "Don't
you touch me!"

Now her head is still down, she still hasn't seen me. I
reached out with my other hand to feel for my friend. And

he wasn't close enough to touch. I said, "Come here, John. Come here."

And he said, "Oral, I've never been confronted with anything like this before."

And I said, "Well, it's a great experience for you."

(I wasn't feeling overly confident myself.) I could feel something going up and down my spine. When I reached forth my hand to touch her, it was like a dozen invisible hands grabbed my hand and manhandled it. Now, something that I could not see took my hand and shoved it back. Apparently, this girl was not moving a muscle — at least that we could see. I kept pressing my hand in until I put it on her forehead. The moment I touched her forehead I spoke in the name of Jesus to the demons. Through the gift of discerning of spirits I was given the number of the demons in her. I was given their names, how long they had been in her, and what they were doing to her. All this came in a flash. Immediately I spoke to the demons — not in my name nor in my strength, but in the name of Jesus of Nazareth — and told them to take their hands off God's property, that that human being was God's. I began to call them out. Now it took 3 or 4 minutes because they didn't all come out at once. It appeared that one would come out, then two or three others would come out. When the prayer was over and Jesus Christ had delivered the girl, she looked up and opened her eyes. I asked her to look at me and when she turned and looked at me, there was a smile, a flood of relief, on her face. I said, "Let me have your hand. I want you to shake my hand." She acted like she was coming out of a coma — out of a trance. I said, "I want you to shake my hand. I am Oral Roberts."

And she said, "You are?"

I said, "Yes."

You see, it wasn't the girl who was recognizing me as I was coming behind her. The recognition was in the demon that was in her, so I introduced myself to her. Then I led her gently out of the car, took her into the auditorium, and gave her to her parents. This is exorcism, or casting out demons in the name of Jesus.

THIS CENTURY HAS PRODUCED A GENERATION OF PSEUDO-INTELLECTUALS WHO DENY THE SUPERNATURAL

The 20th century has produced a generation of pseudo-intellectuals — so-called intellectuals, people that really believe that they *know* something about everything. As a result they have become materialistic and through materialism are trying to live completely on the sense level, denying the intuitive, denying the supernatural — either evil or good — denying the existence of anything supernatural. There has been a repression of belief in spiritual beings and a repression of the belief that we ourselves are spirits, that God made our bodies out of the dust of the ground. We were not a living soul until He breathed the breath of life into us and we *became* a living soul.

Not only that, but in the Resurrection we will be given a new body. In fact, there will be a raising of all the dead, whether they're saved or unsaved, whether they believe in Christ or not. Some will be raised into incorruptible life, into everlasting glory. Others will be raised into everlasting contempt and shame. They'll be given a body that will be cast into a lake of fire in which they will be tormented day and night (1 Corinthians 15; Revelation 20:10-15).

Tormented. Where does that word "torment" come from? It comes from the word "devil." When the archangel Lucifer, of whom we read in Ezekiel 28 and Isaiah 14, was cast out to the earth, followed by his angels, he became the devil. It was the devil (Lucifer) who tried to kill Jesus at His birth. He turned King Herod against the possibility of a new king being born. So King Herod had all the male Jewish babies in the land under 2 years of age killed. It was the devil and his demons that dogged the steps of Jesus everywhere He went. They tried to kill Him in Nazareth.

These spirits are knowledgeable beings. Even though the human eye cannot see them, they are very powerful. Now the difficulty we are having today is in repressing belief in the supernatural, believing that we're just persons of rationalism, that all we can do to solve our problems is through rational thinking, and through the scientific methods only. Although it represses the belief in man concerning these spiritual beings it does not eliminate the spiritual beings. It merely weakens the ability of a person to resist the devil or resist demon spirits. It causes a person to be more open to satanic spirits, to have less resistance. The rise of the occult that we have coming now like a cyclone in this country and throughout the world, is a direct result of man's repression of his normal belief in the supernatural, and particularly because of his denial of God.

I've traveled in all the continents and many nations. I have dealt with thousands and thousands of people of virtually all walks of life and nationalities. Wherever I have gone I have found the belief in the supernatural. I have found the belief in spiritual creatures. I have found a belief in something outside of man. I found it in the American Indians as I have preached to thousands of them. I found it in India. I found it all over Africa. I found it in Russia. The place that I felt more satanic power, more demon power, than any other place in the world was in Moscow. There was a spirit of bondage. It was all over that city.

A beautiful young communist girl, brilliantly educated, was assigned to me and my group as our personal guide for several days. During that time she and I talked about God. She said she was a communist and atheist and did not believe in God. She did not believe in the supernatural. She did not recognize that this is a world of spirits. She did not believe that man was a spirit. She believed man's entire base of existence is an economic base. It begins with a so-called classless society. She began to go into all the things that she had against capitalism and so on. Then she was very courteous and let me talk. I gave my testimony of healing from tuberculosis, of salvation by Jesus Christ, of my belief in the supernatural, my belief in the Resurrection. Immediately, she wanted to know about the Resurrection. She asked me what I thought happened when a person died, and I told her about the resurrection of the dead and how I expected to be raised from the dead when my body died. She said she didn't believe that, that she could not accept it.

I said, "What do you think happens to you when you die?"

She said, "I'll just be dead, that's all."

"Well, what do you mean you'll just be dead?"

"Well, I don't know. I'll just be dead."

You see, she was repeating what somebody had said to her. Then there was a flash of inspiration in my heart and I said to her, calling her by her first name, "You may think you'll be dead, and *just dead*, but you're going to be more alive after death, either as a person indwelt by God or indwelt by Satan, than you've ever been alive on a sense level. As for me, when I die, God's going to raise my body from the dead. I'm going to live in newness of life. I'll have a new body, a glorified body without pain or weakness, and my mind will be perfect. My body will be perfect. I will be, for the first time, a perfect human being — the way God originally made man."

When I finished she brushed the tears back and she said, "Mr. Roberts, you're a happy man. You're a fortunate man." Then she changed the subject.

There's no way that she could get away from a belief in the supernatural because God created man to believe in the supernatural. We're surrounded by a world of spirits, by the angels of God of which there are at least twice as many as there are the angels of the devil. I've always liked that little thought because it is just another evidence that we're on the winning side, you know. You always like to know you're on the winning side of anything.

BRAZIL: DEMON-POSSESSED PERSON DELIVERED

The second incident I want to bring to your mind will illustrate something else about demon spirits. We were in Brazil in 1967 with a group of our own students from the Oral Roberts University World Action Team. We were in Rio de Janeiro in a large auditorium where we were having thousands of people come, both day and night. We had two services a day. This presented a problem in praying individually for the people because there were so many of them. Eventually, before the crusade was over, I pressed my students into service and began to train them — right on the spot — for the ministry of healing of the sick and exorcism of the demon-possessed. One night while a long line of people was coming toward us, I had two students down in front of the platform upon which I was standing. I was directing them as they laid hands on the people and prayed for them and God was using them. As I stood there, just sort of hovering over them and guarding and guiding the best I knew how, I looked over to my left as though pulled by a magnet. There was a man bringing his wife. Immediately through the gift of discerning of spirits, I discerned that she was possessed with many demons.

Now I had dealt with something in this crusade on a larger scale than I'd ever dealt with before. We had a little card on which the person would put his name and address and what he thought was wrong with him — if he were ill spiritually, or physically, or mentally or whatever need there was. Over half of the people would write on their cards *nervousness*. I never had that many people to say they were nervous before but all through the crusade I kept discerning something I couldn't put a name to. That is, I discerned or detected the existence of it but I couldn't put a name to it. Later I was told that more than half the people of Brazil are spiritists who follow after satanic spirits. In one way or another they give themselves to these satanic spirits. It is a religion to them and this had created a nervousness or a condition of imbalance between spirit, mind, and body that they could only describe as *nervousness*. They had no other name for it. So I prayed for them and I had asked God to heal the nervousness but I wasn't getting as much knowledge as I thought I should have to help the people until now.

As this man brought his wife, in a flash I discerned through the Spirit what it was that was tormenting the people. I leaped down from the platform and asked the students to move to my right. I intercepted this man and woman. When she came within 4 or 5 feet of me, the demon spoke. The language down there was Portuguese and I was using an interpreter. The demon in this woman began to speak in Portuguese. She was waving her hands at me and my interpreter was just standing there like he was struck dumb. I said to him, "Interpret to me! What is she saying?"

He was so badly frightened at first that he couldn't open his mouth so I said to him, "Don't be afraid."

I knew it was the demon using her vocal cords but I couldn't get what the words were, so he began to repeat. "You will not cast me out. I will not come out. You cannot cast me out."

Now, after she said that, she lunged toward me. When she lunged toward me she let out sort of a bloodcurdling scream. It was so scary the people who were in the line all around her just fell back. Her husband grabbed her and couldn't control her. She was like a wild beast. I mean, this husband of hers, as big as he was, couldn't hold her. She made several lunges at me and each time she would fall back. There we stood.

I can never be grateful enough in situations like this (where I have normal fear, where the first feeling I have is, *Brother, where's a door? I'm getting out of here!*) for the gift of discerning of spirits. The Holy Spirit's presence makes all the difference.

The first feeling you have is to run because there's danger. But the Holy Spirit brings a calmness — the gift of discerning of spirits just sort of brings light. It opens the area up and the person that is anointed by the Spirit at that time —who is in charge of that meeting—just seems to know. He has a knowing inside him of what's happening.

I saw the condition she was in and I just stood there. She would lunge and fall back, lunge and fall back. Finally I was able to touch her and pray for her. I asked the crowd to bow their heads because when we're dealing with a person that is demon possessed we urge people to be very reverent. Not that bowing of the head is any great thing, but we ask them to do something that will help them get their minds on God, because when a demon comes out he makes two types of efforts:

One, is to get back into the same person. Jesus teaches in Matthew 12 that when the evil spirit comes out of a man he walks through dry or uninhabited places and then he returns with seven more demons — seven more powerful than himself — to try to reenter, and often does. When he does, then the last fate of the person is worse than the first.

Second, is that the demon tries to enter someone else.

I was in the big tent one night in a certain city. We were having a night when it seemed like every third person was demon-possessed. It's like that in this ministry. There'll be nights when there'll be none and then the night comes when it seems like the whole demon world erupts on you. I was urging the crowd, sometimes saying, "Touch the chair in front of you as though you were touching the person. Pray with me. Pray for the person. Pray with me. Fill this room with your faith."

When the demon came out of one person I had prayed for, all of a sudden over to my right at the edge of the tent a man let out a bloodcurdling yell and ran. The demon had struck him and he had entered him. The police ran after him, caught him, and brought him back. We had to pray for him and were able to help him.

I don't want to overdramatize what I'm saying, but if I tell it any other way I'm not really telling it like it is.

I will come back to the woman in Brazil presently but let me interject this: The Spirit of God moves through my hands. When I try to explain that to people I only confuse them, because I can't understand it myself. I just know it and that's it, because He happened to deal with me that way. God may not deal with you that way, or anyone else; it's just His way of dealing with me. The presence of the Lord — the anointing of the Lord — moves through my hand so that I can detect the presence of the evil spirit, to know what his name is, or the number of them. Now sometimes it doesn't work that clearly, but when it does work that clearly I know their number and their name and usually have the power to cast them out. I don't always.

THE GIFT OF DISCERNING OF SPIRITS IS NOT ALWAYS THE POWER OF EXORCISM

It doesn't always carry with it the power to cast out evil spirits. It always carries with it the power to detect the demon, to distinguish the presence of the demon that is there. You can discern the spirit whether it's a good spirit, the Spirit of God; or whether it's a spirit of a demon, the spirit of the devil. That gift will reveal that. But it may take a gift of faith or gift of healing to bring the healing to the individual.

THE GIFTS USUALLY WORK IN CLUSTERS

The gifts of the Spirit usually work in clusters. They are not ordinarily manifested just one at a time. The whole group may be there. I'm for that. But one thing that the gift of discerning of spirits will do, it will tie all the gifts of the Spirit together. The gift of discerning of spirits helps us know what kind of spirit is in a person, what's motivating him. That gift ties all the other nine gifts of the Spirit together.

All right, now back to the woman in Brazil. This demon spoke directly to me and said, "You cannot cast me out. I will not come out."

I admit there was a struggle. We would try and apparently we were defeated. Then while I was praying and calling on the name of Jesus Christ and asking Jesus Christ to command this thing to come out, I saw something that explains a lot of things that's going on in the occult world right now. As if by a giant hand, something struck her body. It was like a fist and you could hear it strike her. It would hit her body. In a moment's time her feet flew out from under her. I mean literally flew out from under her so quickly that for a moment her body was perfectly suspended horizontally between me and the audience. There her body was and we could hear something like sledgehammer blows on her body. Her husband screamed. The crowd screamed. You could almost cut the atmosphere with a knife. Then in the same instant that we saw her suspended this invisible power jerked her to the floor with a force that would have ordinarily burst or cracked her skull. You could hear the sound of her body hitting the floor throughout a building that seated 14,000 people. She lay as though she were dead and my first human thought was, *the demons have killed her*.

But you know, the Scripture is usually the thing that will save every situation. That's what Jesus used. I remembered Mark 9 where it says that devils tore a little boy's body. It tore his body and rent him sore and the little boy fell to the ground. Read the 9th chapter of Mark's Gospel about this little boy that the father had brought to Christ. He first brought him to the apostles and they failed and then when Christ appeared, the father said, in essence, "If You can, help me." And Jesus said, "If thou canst believe, all things are possible to him that believeth." The fact is that the demons, as they were being called out of this little boy, rent him *sore*. I mean they beat this little boy's body and they tore at his flesh.

Now when you read of a human body being suspended like that, it could be a trick; it could be a human manipulation but whenever it is not that, it is, in my opinion, a demon. And wherever a demon is at work, it's a satanic atmosphere. It's an atmosphere of destruction.

Then I reached down, precisely as Jesus did in the Bible, and took the woman's limp hand, and began to gently lift her, saying, "In the name of Jesus Christ of Nazareth, rise and be whole." With the same force that she went to the floor she bounded up. It was a complete transformation of a human being by the Spirit of God. That crowd stood to their feet and clapped their hands and shouted for joy. It was a complete change of the spirit of the crusade. In fact, that crusade ended in a blaze of glory that I'll never forget as long as I live. The woman's healing was the key to all of it.

CAN A CHRISTIAN HAVE A DEMON SPIRIT?

I was in Denver in a crusade, and the chairman of the sponsoring pastors brought a woman from behind the platform and into the healing line and asked me to pray for her. He said he'd had a rather difficult time with her (which was the understatement of a lifetime). I didn't think any more about it until he brought her into the line and stood by her side. I later knew why he stood there — he knew I was going to need help. She was a rather large woman. She must have been 5'-9" tall, very heavy built and apparently very, very physically strong. She had been a missionary to Africa. Now she was home. She had been sent home by the mission board. There were times when she was uncontrollable. She was very destructive. This, of course, had not been told to me. I was just told that he had a woman whom he'd been having a difficult time with, who had been attending his church.

I put forth my hand to touch her forehead and started praying. When I did, she erupted. She just took my hands and arms and threw them up. Then she reached over and took me by the coat. . . Now, I'm sitting on a chair on the platform. She's standing down on the ground in front of me. She reached up and got me and in one motion she just physically lifted me off my chair. I weigh 185 pounds but she physically lifted me and threw me on the ground. Well, I picked myself up and looked around. I tell you, I've known people with great physical strength but nothing like this. The buttons on my coat flew in very direction, my shirt was ripped open.

It was at that moment that I realized what I was up against. The gift of discerning of spirits was in me like a flash. I looked at her and this all began to come out. In Africa, she had been alone. Somebody had made the mistake of putting her with a tribe where witchcraft was highly practiced. The witchdoctors were extremely powerful and she had gotten involved, probably at first through curiosity.

I think everybody is curious about spiritual things, whether it's God or the devil. We're just incurably religious. We are made as spiritual beings and probably she had gotten curious and had taken a step or two to see what it was all about and got involved to the extent that now she gets carried away with the power of this witchdoctor. After awhile the power of Jesus Christ is not working in her. Now, apparently, this is what happened and she has this urge to destroy people. It's an overwhelming thing. It's like a hex has been put upon her. It's like a spell has been cast on her. It's a spirit of evil.

It's really a puzzling question when I'm asked, "Can a Christian have a demon spirit?" My first answer is, "No, absolutely no! There's no way a demon can cross the bloodline!" YET, IF A PERSON TURNS AWAY FROM CHRIST, HE LEAVES A VOID. It's like Jesus taught in Matthew 12 that when the demon comes out — the house is empty, swept, and cleaned up. But then the devil tries to come back and he comes back with reinforcements. Unless the person goes on with God, he apparently opens himself up. So I don't know that I can give you as good an answer as I'd like to give. I can give you a very honest and frank one but I don't know that it's a very satisfactory answer.

Anyway, when I stepped toward this woman to touch her the second time, she just picked me up and tossed me back as though I were a little baby. I have never felt such superhuman strength. Finally, she ripped my coat off. My cufflinks are gone. She's tearing my shirt off my back. There are thousands of people watching this. There's a gasp in the crowd. I mean, people are frightened. Then there was a moment when it was so quiet you could almost hear the quietness. I was all alone, or I felt I was, dealing with a power that apparently was going to rip my body apart. The main thing the demon was doing was not letting me touch the woman. Every time I would move my right hand toward her she would just toss me back. The Spirit cleared my mind and gave me presence of mind to where I knew what was happening.

She and I began a duel, I mean I would put my hand forward and she would put hers forward. I would jerk mine back and finally I was able to get my hand on her forehead. She had her hands on my hand but she could not pry my hand loose. When she could not pry my hand loose, I knew that the Spirit of God had taken control. I mean I knew that battle would soon be over. I was speaking through the Spirit. (The microphone was near enough where the crowd could hear me.) The Spirit was telling me how many years this had been going on and the type of demon it was, the number, and names of the demons.

Then I began through Christ's name to exorcize the demons, to call them out. They were demons of sadism, demons of destruction whose only satifaction was to destroy, to hurt someone. When the demons came out, it was probably the most dramatic moment of my entire ministry. You could hear them come out. You could hear the gurgling sound in her throat. You could hear them in the atmosphere as they were moving about. The crowd knew it; I knew it. Then, all at once, her face shone like an angel. She looked at me and said, "Brother Roberts, Brother Roberts, I'm free! I'm free! Jesus Christ has set me free!"

I don't know whether you believe in oldtime shouting religion or not, but I'm telling you we shouted for joy. I mean it was great. I said to the chairman, "Pastor, here she is."

They walked off triumphantly together. I was so spent I had to close the service. There wasn't anything else I could do for anybody.

I'm sure I still haven't answered, to your satisfaction, the question, "Can a demon enter a Christian?" My answer simply is: Certainly not if he is a Christian who follows Christ. But if we turn away from God . . . if we get involved in things that are not of God, apparently things like this can, and do happen. This is why it is so terribly important to stay close to Jesus and serve Him as your Lord and Savior.

Aerial view of the Oral Roberts University campus. Inset — the new Worship Center on the ORU campus.

CHAPTER TEN

THE MIRACLE OF ORAL ROBERTS UNIVERSITY AND HOW IT WAS BUILT FROM NOTHING

"ORAL, YOU CAN'T DO IT!"

This emphatic warning came from a warm friend of many years, and the pastor of one of our great churches in Tulsa. I knew that his words were really a sincere, earnest plea. What he was really saying was, "Oral, don't try it . . . it's bigger than you are . . . I don't want to see you make a fool of yourself."

My friend was talking about the building of Oral Roberts University. We were starting to build—with NOTH-ING. We have never had any tangible assets to start a major building and when we announced that we were going to build, people were fearful — including my friend. It just simply didn't look possible.

And from the standpoint of human reason my building a first-rate liberal arts university couldn't be done. But these people had no idea of what was inside me. I've never done anything of a major nature until God spoke to me. I'm not saying that He speaks to me every time in a loud voice bu when He speaks to me it's clear enough that I understand Him. I don't take any steps — that is, initiated by myself —

unless I hear from God. And I've always believed in doing things first-rate for God.

I'm very fortunate that right after my conversion my mother kept saying to me:

"Oral, obey God."

She just drilled it into me . . . "Obey the Lord; obey the Lord; obey the Lord." Now this is how you begin to get needs met in your life . . . by obeying the Lord. I know. I've been down that road. The HOW is not important. The how will come. The important thing is to KNOW that the Lord is dealing with you and that the Lord wants you to do something.

When I was just a young man God had said — and I heard the words deep inside myself —

"BUILD ME A UNIVERSITY . . . BUILD IT UNDER THE AUTHORITY OF GOD AND ON THE HOLY SPIRIT"

And God said, "I will let you build it out of the same ingredient I used when I made the earth — NOTHING."

Can you imagine how I felt . . . having God say this to me when I was just 17? I didn't understand . . . but I carried this dream in my heart, never doubting He wanted me to do it. I entered the ministry and in 1947 began this worldwide ministry of deliverance. All through those years of traveling in all the continents of the world, of preaching to the masses, of being on national television and radio, it was in my mind . . .

"BUILD ME A UNIVERSITY . . ."

Of course I often wondered why God wanted ME to build a university. I had gotten through high school after I was healed of tuberculosis. I went to college but only finished 3 years because my time had come to pray for the sick, and I had to go.

I RAN OUT OF TIME
SO I NEVER GRADUATED FROM COLLEGE

I'm the only man at ORU on the faculty who has not graduated from college . . . and over half of my faculty have earned doctorates. I've had to make up for it by studying hard outside of college. So I questioned, why would God want a man in the healing ministry to build a university?

Then I began to understand as God revealed to me that He wanted me to bring healing to the whole man — spirit, mind, and body. And He wanted an education for the whole man — mind, spirit, and body. I knew that man was more than mind . . . he was more than spirit . . . he was more than physical — he was all three. He was like a circle. Anytime you touch a part of a circle you touch all of it. Whenever you touch a human being at any place in his existence, you have touched all of him because you cannot separate his triune of being. When God said to build a university and do it for the education of the whole man, I knew it would take the power of the Holy Spirit.

In my heart, God kept saying:

"BUILD ME A UNIVERSITY . . . THE HOW WILL COME . . . BUILD IT."

In 1952 I drove by the property that is now the campus. My children were with me. I looked over the property and I prayed, "God, hold this land for us to build Your university on."

The land was owned by an oil family. A number of people had tried to buy it, but this family was so rich that they didn't need to sell. But in 1962 I felt impressed of the Lord to send our attorney to them to try to buy the land. And they said, "Yes, we'll sell it — we decided to yesterday." So we paid down on the land, borrowed some money, dug some holes and began to lay the foundations for the first buildings. We had no money, no faculty, no students; and nobody believed that we could do it.

OUR PERSONAL COMMITMENT TO ORU

I had continued on the "love-offering plan" as a means of personal support until about 1960. At that time, my wife Evelyn and I felt directed to go on a set salary. We decided to give what we had saved over the years to ORU. After much prayer I discussed this with my team, then with the Board of Trustees of our Evangelistic Association.

With everyone understanding the decision, I went on a set salary. I have been just as happy as I was before. I have learned that in order to progress a Christian has to change, not in principle but in method. It is not always easy to do but it is absolutely necessary for growth in Christ.

A DAY OF TRIUMPH

On September 7, 1965, we welcomed our first freshman class of 300 to ORU. In my opening address I challenged the students:

In the history of the human family, there has been only one complete whole man. This was Jesus of Nazareth. Our concept of the whole man is derived from His life and from the example He left us. Combining what we know about Him with the most modern techniques of higher education, we have brought into being this new University and through it, we reach for wholeness.

While others are reaching for a ride to the moon, you will reach for a whole life.

ORU is a daring new concept in higher education. It was planned from the beginning to innovate change in all three basic aspects of your being — the intellectual, the physical, and the spiritual.

There's an education here for your mind, for without the development of your intellect you cannot be a complete person.

There's an education here for your body, for that too is essential to your development as a whole person. Jesus is our great example. He personified health and vitality.

There is a unique oportunity here for an education or development of your inner man, for the most important part of you is your spirit.

The world doesn't need more college students to wave flags, carry placards, halt traffic, and riot against law and order. What our civilization needs is that you will make your spiritual development a normal part of your education and your life.

You can emerge as the world's most wanted college graduates. A healthy body that you know how to take care of, a trained and disciplined mind that never settles for less than excellence, governed by an invincible spirit of integrity, inspired by a personal relationship with a living God, and driven by an irresistible desire to be a whole man to make a troubled world whole again!

The second year, 546 students were enrolled.

APRIL 2, 1967, A DAY TO REMEMBER...

One of the great days in our life was the dedication of Oral Roberts University. More than 18,000 people came from all over the United States, Canada, and from several foreign countries to attend the service that lasted a little over 2 hours! The main speaker was my warm friend, Dr. Billy Graham.

The ceremony was to begin at 2:30 p.m. and by noon traffic was backed up for miles in either direction of the 500-acre campus. Not to be outdone by the traffic snarl, hundreds of Tulsans stayed at home to watch the impressive outdoor ceremonies on local television.

Local, as well as national VIP's were on hand to observe firsthand our dream of a lifetime — a high caliber university of academic excellence, where Christ is the center of all learning.

Faithful partners of the Oral Roberts Ministry were present to share the greatness of the moment, with the students they had helped to sponsor, in a setting they had helped to build. They were a part of history and they knew it. This was a day of fulfillment for the ministry they loved. Pride seemed to be bursting at the seams as many expressed their heartfelt sentiments. Several mentioned, "This is the most exciting moment of my life!"

In his dedicatory address Billy Graham said, "This certainly is the university of tomorrow. Evangelical Christendom can be proud today of this university and what it will mean to the future of this country . . . May ORU produce a holy enthusiasm for the will of God. It's still true that people who get excited about the Scriptures and the will of God are people who can change the world . . . To this end we dedicate ORU."

Later Billy said to me, "Oral, be tough with ORU."

I said, "What do you mean, Billy?"

He said, "Be tough with the students and faculty; be tough with your standards and principles; be tough." He added, "That's the only way God will bless the school."

I believe it. I'm dedicated to obeying God so He can use everything about the school to change young lives and set them on fire for the Lord.

THE MIRACLE OF ACCREDITATION

Even before we opened the doors of ORU in 1965 we had already begun the process of receiving accreditation with the North Central Association of Colleges and Secondary Schools. Again the skeptics said, "You can't do it."

I've heard that all my life. "You can't do it . . ." It's like waving a red flag in front of me because God had said, "Build Me a University . . ."

On the other hand, God has His own ways of encouraging me and letting me know that He truly had spoken to me.

A man from Canada, whom I've never met, wrote me a letter. In it was a check. He said:

Oral Roberts,

I'm sending you this money to help build the university on the Holy Spirit. God spoke to me and told me to help a man by the name of Oral Roberts to build Him a university. So here is the money. I don't know why I'm sending it because I really don't like you. But God spoke to me. It's all the money I have.

I called my men together and read the letter to them. There was quite a substantial check in it and we said, "Let's send it back to him if it's all the money the man has. He might go hungry." Then we read the letter again and we saw a deeper meaning. The man was saying to me, "Don't think I sent this money to *you*. I sent it because God told me to send it because He wants a university built on the Holy Spirit. He will take care of me."

As I said, we had begun to apply for accreditation. And they began to lay the rules and regulations down to us . . . you can't do this and you can't do that. We finally reached the point where we stood face-to-face with the people from the North Central Association that accredits the big ten universities and we are in that same district. Face-to-face and toe-to-toe we said, "This is the way we are to build it . . . academically, strong and sound; physically, for the development of our bodies; and spiritually, God first."

"Are you going to teach evolution?" they asked. "Well, yes, we will teach everything that we can find that man has taught about evolution and tell it to our students."

"You will?"

"Yes. But we will also say, 'Now THIS is what we believe.'"

These were great educators — Ph.D.'s — very respectful but very tough, and one of them said, "Well, my idea of a college is that a kid comes here and we throw everything at him we can to try to destroy his faith in God." He said, "Mr. President, what do you have to say to that?"

Before I could answer, Dr. Hamilton, who had just become our dean, said, "Let me answer that. We at Oral Roberts University do not believe that we have a right to destroy anybody's faith in God. Rather, we will try to establish his faith in God."

The chairman of that committee turned to this Ph.D. and said, "You've said enough. Let's talk about something else." So we moved off that subject.

We wound up saying, "This is what we will do. We have met your standards of academics. [We had more than met every standard.] Every building is more than is needed. The library is greater. The Ph.D.'s are more, the program is more. [They admitted that.] But all these other things, that's our business."

And they finally admitted, "It IS your business. Our business is your academic affairs. Your business is what you preach — your philosophy. We will require you, however, to live up to your philosophy."

Inside I was saying, "Thank You, God, thank You. They are going to require us to live up to our spiritual standards." This is the North Central Association of Colleges and Secondary Schools. I mean, you couldn't beat that if you tried. We can't change, because the North Central Association is demanding we live up to our spiritual standards.

So on Wednesday, March 31, 1971 — just 6 short years after the University had opened its doors — we were notified that Oral Roberts University had been granted full accreditation by the North Central Association of Colleges and Secondary Schools. This University is one of the few colleges ever to have achieved full accreditation in this length of time — and one of the very few private institutions ever to be granted the full ten-year term when first accredited, and that, by unanimous decision. It was a day of victory!!! Another miracle!

THE MIRACLE OF OUR ATHLETIC PROGRAMS

I remember when we opened the University in 1965 and announced that we would have a first-class liberal arts university that the skeptics had a field day. And when I began to talk about fielding a basketball team that would compete in national championships, I'm not sure they even listened!!!

But I had a burning call in my soul . . . I knew the Lord had spoken to me. As a young minister, the Lord had said to me, "Go into all the WORLD and preach the gospel . . ." Now the Lord was saying to me, "This also means to go into every man's world." The Lord brought to my mind the 60 million men and women in America who turn first to the sports pages of their newspapers . . . people for whom the sports page almost seems to be their bible. And the Lord impressed me . . .

GO . . . INTO EVERY MAN'S WORLD . . . EVEN INTO THE WORLD OF SPORTS

I got excited when I began to see the possibility of a great witness for Christ through a winning athletic program. I saw in my mind stories of our teams and their Christian witness on the sports pages of America . . . I saw millions reading this witness . . . millions who might not be reached in any other way. So we began. And as usual . . .

WE STARTED WITH NOTHING ! ! !

We had to start from scratch, recruiting for a newly created university which had not even held its first class. We opened that first season (1965-66) with a freshman team, competing against a junior college schedule. That year our basketball team, the "Titans," established a winning tradition by winning almost two-thirds of their games and seeing 4-year colleges on the second year's schedule. The third season (1967-68) found us competing against 4-year colleges and universities . . . several of them listed among the major schools in the country. We closed out that season with a resounding 109-72 victory over a fine team.

That year *Sports Illustrated* carried an article about ORU. It also quoted a big part of my testimony of how God healed me from tuberculosis. How I thank God for that. For without a Christ-centered athletic program at ORU, *Sports Illustrated* never would have carried my testimony or presented us to its millions of readers and fans.

As a result of this article young people wrote us, saying how it had touched them. Also several coaches wrote, saying that they were glad to be reminded of Christ and their need of Him.

Then in 1971 we were granted full membership in the National Collegiate Athletic Association. In the 1971-72 season . . .

SOMETHING ESPECIALLY GOOD HAPPENED TO US!

The season started with four straight narrow victories, (three of them by a total of 5 points) and one loss. What happened after that was unbelievable unless you believe in miracles:

- Titans set a new all-time NCAA scoring record of 105.1 points per game.
- They led the nation in rebounding.
- They received a bid to the National Invitation Tournament. There they defeated Memphis State, champion of the Missouri Valley Conference, in the first round of the National Invitation Tournament played in the famed Madison Square Garden in New York City. And they won by 20 points — 94-74.

You can believe that I was one happy man. Not only for the records that were set but also for the entrance that it gave us on so many sports pages — and on a regular basis. People were beginning to sit up and take notice — not only to stories of our team but also to our television programs. Coaches, as well as many others from across the country who had watched the team play, were interested in learning more about ORU and what I had to say, so they began turning on their TV sets to our programs of the gospel.

In 1972-73 the ORU Titans again set a winning record. One home game was televised nationally by the Hughes Sports Network. And they again played in the National Invitation Tournament at Madison Square Garden in New York City. During the season they played before nearly 200,000 people (if you draw 200,000 people you are one of the top 30 drawing teams in the nation).

And while our basketball team was grabbing headlines, our other teams — baseball, tennis, and golf — were setting records of their own. Each one was — and is — helping us to witness to America's sports-minded millions.

THE MABEE CENTER — ANOTHER MIRACLE

In late 1972 Billy Graham was again on our campus to speak in the first meeting conducted in our new $11-million Mabee Center. We began this building, thinking it would cost $5 million, and we began it with a seed of $232. That is another miracle story all in itself. It was built at a time when the economy of the nation was in trouble. Money was tight . . . and before we finished it was even tighter. But I felt I had to go by the deep feeling I had within that God wanted this building built. It was a building we desperately needed. It's a multipurpose building. Our attendance had grown to such an extent that we had no place large enough on campus to seat all the students. The Mabee Center seats upwards to 13,000 for some events, 11,000 for sports events, and can be divided by special curtains to an auditorium seating 3,000 for dramatic presentations. Here our *Holy Spirit In The Now* class, of which I was privileged to be the first professor, meets each week with an enrollment of over 2,000. (This is the J. Arthur Rank chair of the Holy Spirit, ORU's first endowed chair.) Also our students meet here for their chapel services twice each week. However, by

1975 we will have completed construction on our beautiful new 4,000-seat Worship Center, which I will tell you more about later in this chapter.

Our half-hour television programs and some of our quarterly hour-long Specials are also taped in the Mabee Center.

While Billy Graham was here he said, "It's a great privilege to be back at ORU and to see this magnificent campus. I cannot believe it's the same place that we dedicated 5½ years ago because the changes are absolutely tremendous. I've seen your television programs every Sunday and the quarterly Specials. I've seen pictures of ORU but it doesn't describe one-half of what it is when you come in person and see it." (During his visit Dr. Graham also said, "I have been all over the world; I have preached in some of the most magnificent auditoriums all over the world, from the Nippon Budokan Hall in Tokyo to Madison Square Garden in New York, and this [the Mabee Center] is the most beautiful auditorium I think I've ever spoken in. And I think you ought to be proud of it.")

Today on ORU's 500-acre, $60-million campus, more than 2,200 full-time and several hundred part-time students are enjoying an ultramodern educational facility designed for the development of the whole man. Together, we are helping to fulfill God's command to me. "Raise up your students to hear My voice . . . to go where My light is dim . . . where My voice is heard small."

Our students are selected from the thousands who apply each year for admission. God is sending the cream of the crop in young people. He is sending us Spirit-filled dedicated faculty with excellent academic backgrounds. We are continuing to move forward.

THE WORSHIP CENTER

Once again we are building—this time a chapel and an aerobics building. Each day we face new crises, new needs . . . and each day we have to believe God for new miracles.

Since the beginning of ORU, JESUS has been on the campus — in every classroom, dorm, laboratory, office, the grounds . . . everywhere! But the Word of God tells us:

"Not forsaking the assembling of ourselves together, as the manner of some is, but exhorting one another: and so much the more, as ye see the [evil] day approaching" (Hebrews 10:25).

As we have grown from our first 300 students in 1965 to well over 2,200 full-time students in 1973 (not counting several hundred part-time students) and over 350 staff and faculty, we have managed to assemble ourselves together as a body to worship our Lord together and to have fellowship together as we sit side-by-side in one place. To me, this is what has kept the campus together in the unity of the Body of Christ. We have never compromised the spiritual life and goals to which God has called us. Many students who are enrolled at ORU, either unsaved or not close to God, found a new life in Christ through those chapel services; hundreds have received the infilling of the Holy Spirit and there have been many remarkable healings and miracles. I have had the privilege of preaching the gospel in these services and pouring out my heart to the students. There is nothing that can take the place of these meetings together under the banner of our Lord's love.

Since 1965 I have dreamed of a special building to serve these needs permanently. We have prayed and planned and drawn several different plans, but it was only a few months ago that everything seemed to fall into place, fitting the exact feeling deep within our hearts that said, "This is it . . . it's time to build the Worship Center . . ." That inner knowing that I call *faith* filled us and we knew . . . that we knew . . . that we knew.

In all my ministry through the years when God finally showed me His plan and His time — it's been remarkable how faith would rise within me and I would have this KNOWING . . . and I could speak in Jesus' name to the devil and say:

"Devil, take your hands off God's property . . ." and it would be done! But until I could reach that knowing of faith in my heart, the devil could hinder. But no more on the Worship Center — we're off and running with it for the Lord!

Upon hearing that the Worship Center was soon to be constructed, students came up to me. I vividly remember one group that said, "Brother Roberts, we have seen the need for our very own building in which we could be completely free to worship God in spirit and in truth. We felt He was going to show all this to you. Now that He has, we're just overflowing with His love and joy. We'll do anything to help you. Every day we will pray and expect a miracle." Hundreds of my partners across America have responded . . . So again we are building and with God's help, expect to have our new Worship Center completed by 1975.

THE NEW AEROBICS BUILDING

Physical education is a part of our whole man concept and is required all 4 years in order for a student to graduate.

Recently we have been working toward a new concept in physical education, called "Aerobics." This has been developed by Dr. Kenneth Cooper, a retired air force physician, who has come up with a scientific way wherein physical education and physical development can be measured. He is our official consultant. Although he originally developed this program for the air force, Oral Roberts University will be the first in education to offer a B.S., and eventually a Master's degree in Aerobics.

I believe as the Aerobics program develops at ORU, it will touch the lives of millions of people — adults as well as young people — and will influence all the school systems of America.

Our present facilities are inadequate to house such a program. Hence, we now have under construction an innovation in the area of physical education plants — the Aerobics Building. It will be completed by the fall of this year.

I am continually asked, "How do you support such a tremendous operation as ORU — the buildings, the salaries, the scholarships?" I always reply, "You can't build anything of value with just money; you build with people. People who have faith, people who give as a seed they plant, people who expect miracles. Somehow, when you put first things first, the money comes."

I admit there are months our back is to the wall. Sometimes the devil tempts me to run around telling about all the needs we have. But God calms me down, reminding me who my Source is, asking me if I am giving, and giving first, and if I am expecting miracles from these seeds of faith I plant.

Do you know when you are the strongest? You are the strongest when you're really looking to God, and not to people, as your Source. That's the story of my life and of this ministry of world evangelism — it's looking to God and to Him alone to supply our needs.

It sounds crazy to some people but it's the most scriptural and sensible and workable way there is. I believe it with all my heart.

THE ONE PRAYER I KNOW GOD WON'T ANSWER

Everything in my natural being cries out, "God, let me live knowing where the money is coming from . . ." but I know this is one prayer that God will not answer. I know God is going to hold us here in the open fields of faith —

standing on the frontier of the realm of miracles, with the wind in our face,

looking into an indefinite future,

not knowing where we will get our next dollar, or our next building, or our next professor, or the answer to the next unsolvable problem that will face us but . . .

expecting a new miracle every day from the hand of God.

Evelyn and I in a dialogue concerning the prayer language of the Spirit.

CHAPTER ELEVEN

THE MIRACLE OF
"THE PRAYER LANGUAGE
OF THE SPIRIT"

(The God-given ability to pray
both with your spirit AND with your mind)

IN 1947 WHEN GOD let me know that my time had come
to take His healing power to my generation, my first reaction was . . .

"I DON'T KNOW HOW!!!"

I knew I had been healed myself. I knew that I believed
in God's great healing power — both medical and divine
healing. But I didn't know HOW God was going to use me
because I did not consider myself a gifted person. I struggled with this day and night. During those days of heart-
searching I would often say to God:

"Let me see Jesus Christ with my eyes like the
disciples did . . . like Peter, James, and John did. Let
me SEE Him. Let me have a vision of this Man
physically as they did. Then I can go and pray for
the people. I can go where they are. I can enter into
their sufferings. Otherwise, I don't know HOW."

It was at this point that God spoke to me again. I
heard His voice deep inside me. He said:

"Do you have the baptism in the Holy Spirit?"

And I said:

"Yes." (I had received this charisma — this gift of
the Spirit — shortly after my conversion. I had also spoken
in "tongues" a few times since then.)

Then the Lord said to me:

"Do you know what you have?"

In all honesty I had to reply that I did not.

Then God said. . .

"You said you wanted to SEE Jesus. Well, having the baptism in the Holy Spirit gives you a sense of His physical being as well as His spiritual being. When you have the baptism in the Holy Spirit it's precisely as if Jesus is walking by your side in the flesh. Do you understand that?"

And of course I did not fully understand. No one had ever really explained it to me this way before. So I began a study of the Holy Spirit that was to last until today . . . a study into what it means to be baptized in the Holy Spirit and to speak in tongues . . . which I call *the prayer language of the Spirit*. (I use the terms synonymously — speaking in tongues, the prayer language of the Spirit, and praying in the Spirit — they all mean the same thing.)

I read in the Bible where Jesus said:

It is expedient for you that I go away: for if I go not away, the Comforter will not come unto you; but if I depart, I will send him unto you (John 16:7).

I looked in the Greek and found that in this Scripture the word "Comforter" means PARACLETE. The word "paraclete" is translated *comforter* in the King James Version of the Bible. It means "one called alongside to help . . . one who warns, one who admonishes . . . one who helps us over our rough spots." So the divine Paraclete is one who gives us what we need at the time we need it.

Once when I was teaching on this I called up a member of my class and illustrated it this way.

Roberts: Will you open your billfold a moment, please, and take out a dollar bill?

Student: Yes.

Roberts: OK. I'm going to take your dollar.

Student: I thought you would.

Roberts: But, I'm going to give you another dollar. Will you take it?

Student: Yes.

Roberts: Now that dollar is just as genuine as the one you gave me. It is also printed by Uncle Sam — it's a genuine dollar. Now do you have as much as you had before you gave me your dollar?

Student: Yes.

Roberts: I gave you another dollar. And that dollar has the identical buying power of the dollar you gave me?

Student: That's right.

I want you to notice that when the student gave me his dollar and I gave him back another dollar, he was just as well off as he had been before. In the same way, Jesus was saying to His disciples, in essence:

"If I go away I will send you another Paraclete . . . one called alongside to help. I have been by your side physically. I have been everything to you. Now you are distressed because I'm physically leaving the earth, but if I go back to My Father I will send you another Paraclete."

When Jesus *physically* left from the earth He said He would send us another Paraclete, one called alongside to help, and we would do better with our lives than if He (Jesus) had remained physically with us. I wish you would reread this illustration and think about it until it becomes really clear to you.

So back in Enid, Oklahoma, in 1947, these things were happening in my spirit and understanding. I began to realize —

I DON'T HAVE TO SEE JESUS CHRIST AS A PHYSICAL MAN. JESUS HAS FILLED ME WITH THE HOLY SPIRIT. I HAVE THE COMFORTER, THE DIVINE PARACLETE, THE ONE CALLED ALONGSIDE TO HELP. IT'S AS IF JESUS CHRIST IS WALKING BY ME IN THE FLESH . . . EXCEPT THAT HE IS NOW IN HIS IN-VISIBLE *UNLIMITED* FORM. HE IS *IN* ME; THEREFORE, HE CAN DO THESE THINGS THROUGH ME.

This was the key that opened the lock. This was the beginning of my understanding of the baptism in the Holy Spirit and the prayer language of the Spirit and what it means to have the Holy Spirit working in our lives.

Now this prayer language is a language of the *spirit* — not of the intellect. Your spirit communicates directly with God — without the aid of your mind — through "other tongues" . . . another language that you have never learned . . . a language given you by the Holy Spirit. Your spirit talks to God out of the depths of your inner being. Your spirit is now able to talk to God freely because the Holy Spirit has come in and by the fusion of your spirit with the Holy Spirit (much like your two hands joining together) the "tongues" or the prayer language of the Spirit is produced.

You see, through the fall of man his mind has become blurred. He no longer could see God clearly. As someone has said, man's mind now acts as a censor and too often it censors out what God says to him.

A censor just lets certain things go by. For example, if a prisoner writes a letter, that letter is intercepted by a censor and read; and portions of it may be deleted, so that the person who receives the letter may or may not receive the entire letter as it was written. In the same way, when Jesus was on the earth talking to His disciples they listened to Him, but their minds censored out parts of what He said. Their minds intercepted lots of things that Jesus said, and did not let them get down into their spirit. Therefore, they did not understand what Jesus was saying.

But on the Day of Pentecost when Jesus baptized them in the Holy Spirit and the Spirit got down into their spirit, they were able to speak in another language . . . a tongue that their minds had not learned and did not understand. This new tongue could not be censored by the mind because the mind did not understand what the spirit was saying. So once again man could communicate directly with God from his spirit and mind, as Adam first did.

THE PRAYER LANGUAGE OF THE SPIRIT RESTORES OUR ABILITY TO COMMUNICATE DIRECTLY WITH GOD

As mortals, we cannot look upon God. We are not at ease with God. We cannot talk freely to God. Somehow our understanding, our ability to grasp God, to communicate with Him, to understand life as God intended us to, has been blurred. It has been submerged. Something negative has happened to it.

Adam — the first man — had perfect communication with God. But he lost that full communication with God. As I studied Genesis 3, I learned what happened to Adam's ability to communicate with God and what God is trying to do for us through the prayer language of the Spirit.

Adam and Eve were given the power of choice. They were told not to eat of the tree of the knowledge of good and evil. They could say yes to God or they could say no. The devil came to Eve in the form of a serpent and said:

Yea, hath God said, Ye shall not eat of every tree of the garden? (Genesis 3:1).

And Eve replied:

We may eat of the fruit of the trees of the garden: But of the fruit of the tree which is in the midst of the garden, God hath said, Ye shall not eat of it, neither shall ye touch it, lest ye die (Genesis 3:2,3).

Then the serpent said to Eve:

Ye shall not surely die (Genesis 3:4).

(In other words, "God's not telling you the truth." He's lying to you.)

For God doth know that in the day ye eat thereof, then your eyes shall be opened, and ye shall be as gods, knowing good and evil (Genesis 3:5).

Now when the devil told Eve that she would not die he was telling a half-truth. The devil was referring to man's physical death, while God was talking about the death of man's spirit. God was not referring to the immediate physical death of the body but the death of the living spirit within the human body.

In essence, God said:

"When you eat of the fruit of the tree of the knowledge of good and evil, YOU — the total personality, that integrated human being, that deathless, immortal spirit that I made out of nothing — that part of you will die. That part of you that carries My spiritual and moral likeness, that's going to be erased. It will disintegrate. That's what will happen to you."

Now the tree of the *knowledge* of good and evil had to do with the *mind*. God made man a spiritual being. God made man's spirit to be supreme over his mind and his body.

> God didn't make man physical, He just gave him a body.
>
> God didn't make man mental, He just gave him a mind.

GOD MADE MAN SPIRITUAL ! ! !

God put everything in the spirit that had to do with the life of God. And the spirit then was to use the mind and the body as instruments. Through the spirit man would talk and walk with God and subdue the earth and have his LIFE as a WHOLE person.

You see, God loved man and put him together as a perfect being. But the devil sought to separate man and disintegrate his total personality so that he would lose contact with God and would depend only on his powers of reason. That way the devil could get in and influence man's life. The devil knew if he ever got man to die spiritually, if he was successful in disintegrating the inner part of man that he could cause the spiritual likeness of God to disappear from the spirit of man. Then . . .

> Man would be left with a mind and a body, with the ashes of his spirit scattered around him.
>
> He would be like a pale ghost walking through the world . . . not knowing where he was going . . . not knowing how to talk with God . . . running into problems and not knowing how to solve them . . . getting into the night and not knowing how to create light.
>
> Man would find all kinds of knowledge but would have no wisdom to use it.

A bizarre example of this is Hitler who had all the knowledge Satan could help him find — knowledge that within itself was OK, but with no wisdom of God with which to use it. He plunged the world into war. The same kind of thing happened in other wars like in Vietnam and in the Middle East.

Adam and Eve saw that the tree had to do with their intellect; it had to do with their minds. God had told them that they had the power to say yes, but He also said, in essence, "The day that you eat of the tree you will die . . . your spirit will die . . . the real part of you will disintegrate. It will be dead." (When the apostle Paul talks about being "dead in trespasses and sins" (Ephesians 2:1) this is what he means.)

When Adam and Eve ate of the tree, the Bible says, "They knew . . . " THEY KNEW!!!

This is when the mind took ascendancy over the spirit. For the first time since God had created man out of nothing, the mind becomes boss. It's no longer a servant of the spirit of man. It now begins to suppress the spirit, to put it down until it's like a ghost. It's without life.

When Adam chose to eat of the tree of the knowledge of good and evil he was saying to God, in essence: "I want to do what I want to do. I'm going to elevate my mind and make the pursuit of knowledge the main thing in my life" (Genesis 3). And the SPIRIT OF MAN DIED THAT DAY. His spirit was pushed down and his mind rose up and took charge. The mind became ascendant, or supreme, and from that moment on knowledge has been man's god.

The Bible says, "THEY KNEW . . . " and they went off and hid themselves.

When God came in the cool of the evening to talk with them He said, "Where art thou?" (Genesis 3:9).

And Adam said, "I heard thy voice in the garden, and I was afraid, because I was naked; and I hid myself" (Genesis 3:10).

Adam meant that he had discovered that he was mortal and he had not known that before. He knows now that he is mortal, and he became frightened. He discovered that he couldn't look upon God as he once had . . . he couldn't talk with God as he had in the past. So he hid. He covered himself. And man has been afraid of God ever since that time. *In his mortality man has not been able to bridge the gap between immortality and mortality.*

But when man chose to eat of the fruit of the tree of the knowledge of good and evil, God set about to redeem man. He told Eve that He would take of her Seed and that Seed would bruise the devil's head (Genesis 3:15).

> *And I will put enmity between thee and the woman, and between thy seed and her seed; it shall bruise thy head* . . . (Genesis 3:15).

I want you to notice that God said when the Messiah would come that He would deal with the HEAD of the devil. He would deal directly with the INTELLECT of the devil. He would approach the devil on his own ground just as the devil had approached man on an intellectual basis, tested him at the point of his brain — or his mind power — and succeeded in wrestling the control of the mind from under the control of the spirit. God saw this and He said to the devil that the Seed of the woman would bruise his HEAD. Then God also said to the devil:

> *and thou shalt bruise his heel* . . .

Or, in essence, "You'll be able to kill Him" — referring now to Jesus' death on the cross. You know, they never killed Christ. They killed Jesus. Jesus is the human part of the man and Christ is the divine part. They killed the human part — Jesus. The divine part — the Christ — said, "Father, into thy hands I commend my spirit" (Luke 23:46). The devil never got his hands on the Christ. He got his hands on the physical part — the heel — but God said, "the Seed of the woman" — the Christ — "will bruise your head."

Ever since the cross the devil has been a schizophrenic. He doesn't know what is going on. And no one can ever do anything with knowledge alone. If you had all the knowledge in the world, you couldn't cut it. You could not put one marriage together again and make it work. You couldn't solve one problem to the benefit of the deepest level of your being.

Knowledge *by itself* is not an end. It cannot solve anything . . . it has to have something greater than it is . . . the wisdom of God. To have the wisdom of God you must be reawakened by the Holy Spirit and born again . . . until the spirit with which God made you . . . comes alive and you become a living soul again.

THE HOLY SPIRIT NOW LIVES WITH YOU ! ! !

When you are converted (saved, born again, accept Christ — these terms all mean the same thing) the Holy Spirit brings you to Christ. The Holy Spirit gives you a new birth. In the same way that the Holy Spirit conceived Jesus, you are born again. You are born the first time of the flesh of your parents but now you must be born the second time of the Holy Spirit. Why? Because that spirit of yours is not alive. Your spirit has to be born again . . . it has to come into existence a second time. Jesus said:

> *Verily, verily, I say unto thee, Except a man be born again, he cannot see the kingdom of God* (John 3:3).

How do we have this experience? The Bible says:

> *Repent, and be baptized every one of you in the name of Jesus Christ for the remission of sins, and ye shall receive the gift of the Holy Ghost* (Spirit) (Acts 2:38).

REPENT. The word "repent" means "to change your mind." I want you to notice how this all goes back to the mind of man. What happened in the Garden of Eden back there was that man chose something, mentally. Man used his mind to choose knowledge. When God sent the Messiah, Christ, He was to bruise the *head* or the *mind* of the devil. So when the Bible tells us to repent, it literally means to change our MINDS.

God doesn't tell you to change your spirit because your spirit is dead. In order for God to get into your spirit you must open your mind and change it. HOW? By saying, "I am wrong." These are the three hardest words that you will ever say . . . "I am wrong." Repentance means "I am wrong."

Not only must you say "I am wrong," as a first act to be born again but you must also continue to say it the rest of your life. You must live in a state of repentance because you will be wrong again . . . and again . . . and again . . . and again!!! And so will I. Repentance begins with the MIND. The Holy Spirit renews your mind.

> *Be not conformed to this world: but be ye transformed by the renewing of your mind* (Romans 12:2).

Jesus Christ became the second Adam. His purpose was to liberate you and me, to bring us into a union with God . . . beginning with our spirit. Jesus came so that the mind which took dominance and supremacy over the spirit and the body and made knowledge its pursuit in life, could now resubmit itself to God. In this way the spirit of man could become dominant and supreme again. Man could once again become a spiritual being.

He would be able to discern spiritually.

He would be able to understand spiritually.

He would be able to see that every problem he has begins in his spirit and every solution to that problem begins in his spirit.

Through the power of the Holy Spirit indwelling us we are discovering that no matter what the problem feels like, it originates in our spirit. It may seem to be a mental or physical or financial or marital or some other kind of problem, but it all begins in our spirit. But, thank God, that's where the answer also begins — in our *spirit*.

ONE OF THE WORKS OF THE HOLY SPIRIT IN YOUR LIFE IN THE NOW IS TO HELP YOU WITH THE THINGS THAT YOU FACE AS A HUMAN BEING.

The apostle Paul, who gave us most of the teaching that we have on the Holy Spirit, said:

Likewise the spirit also helpeth our infirmities

(our weaknesses, our problems, our needs)

for we know not what we should pray for as we ought. (We just don't know how to pray. That is, our mind, our intellect, doesn't have this power. The mind is not a creator. It is only an instrument of the spirit. The creative part of us is in our spirit.)

But the Spirit itself maketh intercession for us with groanings which cannot be uttered. And he that searcheth the hearts knoweth what is the mind of the Spirit, because he maketh intercession for the saints according to the will of God (Romans 8:26,27).

When we reach the place that we just don't know how to pray . . . or the words to say . . . or even what to ask God for, we must not surrender. We must not give up and sit back and say, "It's hopeless." We must not say, "I can't do it." We must understand that within us is the Holy Spirit.

THE HOLY SPIRIT RESIDES DEEP DOWN INSIDE YOU

He is like a river of living water. And He's there flowing 24 hours of the day. Jesus said:

> *If any man thirst, let him come unto me, and drink. He that believeth on me, as the scripture hath said, out of his belly shall flow rivers of living water. (But this spake he of the Spirit, which they that believe on him should receive: for the Holy Ghost was not yet given; because that Jesus was not yet glorified)* (John 7:37-39).

Then Paul said, "He that searcheth the hearts knoweth what is the *mind* of the Spirit . . . " The Holy Spirit is a Person. As a Person, He talks. He has an intellect, and in the mind of the Holy Spirit is all knowledge. In the Holy Spirit's mind is the understanding of all languages. In the Holy Spirit's infinite mind is the ability to communicate with God. So the Holy Spirit searches our hearts and finds what it is that is troubling us.

THE HOLY SPIRIT'S GREATEST FUNCTION IS TO INTERCEDE FOR YOU THROUGH THE PRAYER LANGUAGE OF THE SPIRIT ACCORDING TO THE WILL OF GOD

He really wants to pray in your behalf and to enable you to enter into His prayer for you. The Holy Spirit is within you and He's down there searching your heart . . . searching out what the real problem is . . . searching for that thing that you feel deep down inside on the gut level of life which Jesus called the belly, or the inner man.

THE HOLY SPIRIT GOES INTO THE DEEPEST LEVEL OF YOUR BEING . . .

> finding things that may have started when you were only 3, 6, or 10 years old . . .
>
> finding things that you were hung up on when you were in your teens . . .
>
> finding something way back in your marriage that hurt you . . .
>
> finding that problem that was so severe it looked like it would strangle you to death and crush you out of existence . . .

That thing is there and with all of your praying with your mind, your intellect, you've not been able to bring it up. You've not been able to locate that thing that is troubling you, and to pray according to the will of God for it. Now the mind of the Spirit finds that problem and gathers all that up and begins to pray, to intercede with God, according to the will of God for you.

The Holy Spirit prays in your behalf according to God's will in tongues . . . in words that you've not developed or created. Now in order to pray in tongues, all you have to do is to shut your mind and open your mouth. Give your mind a little rest and start praying with your spirit in the prayer language of the Spirit.

In 1 Corinthians 14:13-15 Paul tells us more about communicating with God through tongues or the prayer language of the Spirit. He says:

> *If I pray in an* **unknown** (this is a translator's word — **unknown** is not in the original text) *tongue, my spirit prayeth, but my understanding is unfruitful.*

That is, my mind is not entering into this thing at all because it doesn't know how — it doesn't know what to pray for. The "tongue" Paul speaks of here is the prayer language of the Spirit.

What is it then? I will pray with the spirit . . .
Or, Paul says, "I'm going to let this new tongue — this tongue created not by my intellect . . . not words that I have learned — I'm going to join the Holy Spirit as He prays in my behalf. I'm going to say those words as He gives me the ability. I'm going to pray in the prayer language of the Spirit."

and I will pray with the understanding also.
Paul explains that after he has prayed in the prayer language of the Spirit that he pauses and asks God to reveal to him what his prayer was and what God's response is so that his mind can understand also (1 Corinthians 14:13).

Praying in the prayer language of the Spirit and then praying with the understanding also puts us at least partially on the level with Adam. Our spirit and mind are no longer strangers . . . they are brothers, they belong together. They are now one unit again. Now, through the power of the Holy Spirit, we can pray with the Spirit AND we can pray with the understanding. Now, we get on a level where we can understand God, where we lose our fear, where we can talk with Him and walk with Him in a different way than we ever have before. We can become truly creative. We can discover new knowledge. We can come into a oneness with God and into a love with one another. We can come into a renewing of our minds by the Holy Spirit.

A PERSONAL EXAMPLE

Let me give you an example from my own experiences of praying with the Spirit and with the understanding also. I shared some of this with you in the previous chapter but it best illustrates my point here. When I began to build Oral

Roberts University back in the early '60s I was confronted with two or three limitations: one, my own inability. I didn't know how to build it but God told me to build it. Now how are you going to do something that God tells you when you don't know HOW?

Secondly, God told me to build the University out of the same ingredient He used when He made the world — and He made it out of NOTHING. So He told me to build Him a university and to build it out of nothing. This may sound funny to you. But believe me, it wasn't funny to me.

Just after I was healed and converted, at the age of 17, God said to me:

"SOME DAY YOU ARE TO BUILD ME A UNIVERSITY. YOU ARE TO BUILD IT ON MY AUTHORITY AND ON THE HOLY SPIRIT."

At age 17, I didn't even know the meaning of those words . . . Me! Oral Roberts who never got to finish college was to build God a university — on His authority and on the Holy Spirit.

So in 1947 God thrust me into a healing ministry that spread all over the world. He gave me a concern for people, a feeling for them. Then in the early '60s God told me the time had come to build the university. "How do I build a university?" I asked. "I'm in the healing ministry. My ministry is even put down by the educators. I'm at the lowest rung on the ladder. I finished 3 years of college but I never graduated. And now I'm going to build a university and I don't even know what one is. I'm just a reasonably intelligent man and I have a gift of God in my life to win souls, to pray for the healing of sick humanity and that's all I have."

But God said, "Your time has come. Build Me a university. Build it on My authority and on the Holy Spirit."

Nobody understood me when I said I was to do this and nobody believed I could do it.

In my heart, God was saying:

"Build Me a university and build it on the authority of God and on the Holy Spirit."

My heart was saying:

"Yes, yes."

And my mind was saying:

"No, No."

Now have you ever had this experience? You see, we had no land, no campus, no buildings, no students, no faculty, no money, and a man who had not finished college . . . and he's going to build a university??? No wonder the skeptics had a field day. Even my own intellect was saying, "You dumb-dumb! ! !"

But thank God for the baptism in the Holy Spirit and the prayer language of the Spirit. By this time I had learned — like Paul — to pray with my spirit and to pray with my understanding also. I would first pray in tongues then I would pause and interpret back to my mind, or with my understanding.

One day I was walking across a piece of land which hopefully would some day be the campus of Oral Roberts University. I was praying in my understanding — that is, in my own language, and getting nowhere. My mind said:

"NO! NO! NO! NO! NO! . . . YOU CAN'T DO THIS ! ! !"

Then I shifted — by my will — and began to pray in tongues and my heart began saying:

"Yes! Yes! Yes! Yes! Yes! You can.

"You will.

"You can.

"You will."

Then this knowing was transferring to my understanding. It came out of my belly — my inner man — it came up like a river. It came up into my mind AND I SAW IT. My mind began to blossom, to sharpen, to come alive to what God was saying to me. All at once — believe me, Friend, when I say this — I understood cnough to build a university. I didn't understand all the details but I understood the basics. I saw that this healing ministry had been born for a purpose . . . including praying for people's bodies and souls . . . but much more . . . it was a ministry to the TOTAL-ITY OF MAN'S NEEDS. I saw that God could reintegrate the total personality of man. I saw that we would create a higher education for your sons and daughters and mine where they would be educated in the spirit, in the mind, and in the body. They would get a *TOTAL* EDUCATION. I SAW IT—

I SAW THE WHOLE MAN CONCEPT AS BASED ON GOD'S AUTHORITY AND ON THE HOLY SPIRIT.

The miracle of the prayer language of the Spirit is a part of my everyday life. For each day I face problems either in the television ministry or in answering people's letters — trying to find God's answer for them — or at the University with the more than 2,000 students, or in the other outreaches of this ministry, or in my personal life. There are problems that I cannot find the answers for . . . but I know that the Holy Spirit can. When I rely on my own understanding I make a lot of mistakes. But when I exercise the gift of the prayer language of the Spirit I discover that I come up with better answers . . . better solutions . . . answers that help us to move forward in taking this message of God's healing power to our generation, and answers for problems I face in my personal life.

QUESTIONS FREQUENTLY ASKED ABOUT THE HOLY SPIRIT . . . AND SPEAKING IN TONGUES

(Note: For several semesters I taught a course on *The Holy Spirit In The NOW* at Oral Roberts University. Often at the close of my lecture I asked my wife Evelyn to join me in a discussion. These questions and answers are taken from some of those discussions.)

Evelyn: I have often heard you say that according to John 7:37-39 and Acts 2:38, when a person repents of his sins and believes on Jesus that he receives the gift of the Holy Spirit. Is this the same as the baptism in the Holy Spirit?

Oral: When you accept Christ as your personal Lord and Savior, of course you receive the Holy Spirit, for without the Holy Spirit himself you are none of His. But there is a baptism in which you are submerged in the Holy Spirit. It's an extra dimension. Jesus referred to it as the rivers of the Holy Spirit flowing up out of your belly — your innermost being (John 7:38,39). Of course the tongues, the new language of prayer and praise, are in that river as it flows up. They are in the baptism, the immersion of you, in the Holy Spirit.

Evelyn: What is the purpose of the baptism in the Holy Spirit?

Oral: Before I answer this question I want to give some background. The Bible says that God made man in His image. That is, we are made in the moral likeness of God. God is not speaking of a physical shape. He was talking about His spiritual and moral likeness. God is pure, which is the way He made Adam and Eve. God is Love; God is Truth. That's how He made us. But by man's rejection of God and by our hurting one another, too often with malice, we have thrust God out of our lives. That is why we have to be born again by the Holy Spirit. God is trying to restore His moral and spiritual likeness, His truth, His life, His values to us, inside.

Evelyn: Does this mean, then, that our spirit inside will be remade in the image of God?

Oral: When God saves us, we are made a new creation (2 Corinthians 5:17). This is the work of the Holy Spirit. But the baptism in the Holy Spirit has a different purpose altogether. Its purpose is *communication with God.* It is to open up the heart, the inner man, which is all too often closed up by hurts, lack of understanding, and our own intellect. Also we don't always know how to pray. The baptism in the Holy Spirit gives a person a new prayer language so he can communicate directly with God. He can edify or build himself up inside spiritually. His intellect blossoms and he can understand God better, also his own purpose in life better.

Evelyn: Often when I mention the baptism in the Holy Spirit and speaking in tongues people say, "But how can I reconcile 1 Corinthians 13:8-10 and speaking in tongues?"

Oral: This is one of the most serious questions I have ever been asked. In 1 Corinthians 13, the love chapter, Paul said:

> *Charity* (love) *never faileth: but whether there be prophecies, they shall fail; whether there be tongues, they shall cease; whether there be knowledge, it shall vanish away. For we know in part, and we prophesy in part. But when that which is perfect is come, then that which is in part shall be done away.*

So the real question is, *Have tongues ceased?* To be absolutely objective and take it like the Bible says, then we have to say no. If you say tongues have ceased, then objectively and honestly you have to say that prophecy has ceased, also all knowledge — and we know these have not ceased.

First, Paul said, "For we know in part." That is why we now pray in tongues. We don't know fully how to pray. We only know partly how to prophesy and we only know part of knowledge. Not even all of us compositely have all knowledge.

But, Paul continues, "When that which is perfect is come, then that which is in part shall be done away." When our Lord comes — and that is what I think this means — He is the Truth, He is the Light, He is all wisdom, He is all knowledge. We will be face-to-face with Him. We will not need to speak in tongues.

Evelyn: Would you say that the Holy Spirit now illuminates our minds, but when Jesus comes we won't need to speak in tongues to get our minds illuminated?

Oral: Yes, because He will be here face-to-face with us. For example, if Jesus Christ were sitting in your chair, do you think I would speak in tongues to Him?

Evelyn: No. You wouldn't need to. So, in other words, the Holy Spirit is to help us get through to Him while we are on this earth.

Oral: Yes, this earth! This life! Before our Lord returns to this earth and before we get to heaven. The baptism in the Holy Spirit is for the NOW.

Evelyn: Today there are many Christians who are open to receiving the baptism in the Holy Spirit. How can we help them receive this gift?

Oral: First of all, I usually ask a person like this, "Do you know Jesus Christ as your personal Savior? Have you repented of your sins and believed on our Lord? Have you committed your life to Him?" Remember that Christ is in your life only by the Holy Spirit. Jesus said that rivers were flowing up; they are flooding up (John 7:37-39). That is, you feel this flooding up in the pit of your stomach. So when you feel this, begin to worship the Lord; and as you do, just open your mouth and stop talking in your own tongue and let the sound come out — you will speak in tongues.

Evelyn: The other day a lady said to me, "How can I know the tongues I speak are by the utterance of the Holy Spirit?"

Oral: There are many good ways for you to determine that when you speak in tongues it is by the utterance of the Holy Spirit. First, it all starts with Jesus. Have you repented of your sins? Have you believed on Him as your personal Savior? Are you seeking Jesus Christ?

Second, when you speak in tongues do you feel an edification of your inner self? a release? a therapy of your inner being?

Every time I pray in tongues I receive a release. There is a quickening, a release of the inner self. That is good. When you are going through some experience that is beyond you — a problem which you just don't have the answer to — about the only way you can get release is to pray in tongues.

Third, your understanding is helped. When you pray in tongues, or sing in tongues, or praise God in tongues; you can pause and ask God to let you interpret.

Let him that speaketh in an unknown tongue pray that he may interpret (1 Corinthians 14:13).

You can interpret your own tongue. You can edify yourself in your spirit and you can also illuminate your mind as a result of praying in tongues.

I do this all the time. I pray and praise God in tongues and then wait a moment and start praying again in my own tongue. Usually the very same words, or at least the understanding of what I have just prayed in tongues, will come to my mind and then my mind can pray better.

Evelyn: Oral, do you think the devil can speak in tongues?

Oral: Unquestionably, no! The devil can't speak in tongues because the Bible says in Acts 2:4, "They . . . began to speak with other tongues, as the SPIRIT gave them utterance." And the Holy Spirit never gives the devil utterance. The devil hates Jesus Christ. He hates the Holy Spirit. And the baptism in the Holy Spirit has to do with Jesus himself. The Holy Spirit's entire ministry is built around Jesus, whom the devil hates.

Evelyn: Someone asked me if speaking in tongues is a result of emotion, or does it bring about emotion? I personally think it causes the emotion. Because when you speak in tongues you must exercise your will and know that you are talking to God, and there is a joy that hits you down inside . . . and joy is an emotion. What do you say?

Oral: Sometimes it is not joy that hits you. Sometimes it is something else. For example, if you are going through a tremendous personal traumatic experience and you begin to pray in tongues, although you feel something inside, it isn't always joy. It's a struggle, strain, burden — sometimes deep sorrow. You may have lost a loved one. There may be a problem in the marriage in which the marriage is dissolving. Remember, we prayed with a dear person the other day whose marriage is dissolving. And she would reach way down where the Spirit of God is and take hold of that sorrow that was breaking her up — a marriage that she has had all these years and suddenly it is going. Later she felt joy when she had emptied herself out and the Spirit began to move in her. She felt joy in that God was with her and she knew God was going to help her. She may or may not solve that marriage problem. But something marvelous happened to her, Evelyn, and *is* happening to her. She has a sense that God is with her and God is going to help her. We don't know what the outcome will be, but we know God is going to help her.

Evelyn: Will the baptism in the Holy Spirit and speaking in tongues mean I will solve all my problems?

Oral: No. The difference is that when you receive the baptism in the Holy Spirit and speak in tongues, your approach to problems will be different. You will have help in the form of an inner release. You will have help in your intellect if you know how to pause and wait for the interpretation. The problems will still be there but you will see them in a different light. You will have to fight them just exactly like you did before you received this gift but you will have very special help in facing those problems.

Evelyn: I am a very practical person. To me, an experience has to be practical or it doesn't do me any good. I believe the infilling of the Holy Spirit can make you more effective in any area of life — He is sent to give you the abundant life in the NOW of your existence.

Oral: I can say AMEN to that.

The Prayer Tower in the center of the Oral Roberts University campus.

CHAPTER TWELVE

THE PRAYER TOWER–
A TWENTIETH-CENTURY MIRACLE

THE DOOR TO THE PRAYER TOWER on the Oral Roberts University campus opened slowly. A young man stuck his head in and said, "Man! Is this place for real?" "Come on in," the Prayer Tower guide responded.

Hesitantly, the young man stepped inside. "I'm from Los Angeles," he explained, "and I was just driving down the road when all of a sudden this place popped up. This is something else — what is it?"

"You're in the Prayer Tower and this is Oral Roberts University," the guide explained. "And it's for real."

Actually, the Prayer Tower on the Oral Roberts University campus is the most "real" thing about the University. It is the spiritual hub of the ORU campus. Here, in the geographical center of the campus the Prayer Tower rises 200 feet into the air like a twentieth-century cross. The "Crown of Thorns" around the observation deck is symbolic of our desire to reach out in all directions of the earth to a needy world. At the very tip of the tower is a flame of fire which symbolizes the Holy Spirit. On the outside, one thousand shining shields of faith mirror the blue of the heavens by day and reflect the glittering stars by night.

Approximately halfway between the base of the tower and its flame is the pulse and the thrust of this ministry — the Abundant Life Prayer Group.

Prayer has been the power and heartbeat behind this ministry since it began in 1947. But because of its phenomenal growth we found that we could not keep up with the many calls of distress that came into the office daily. Thus, the Abundant Life Prayer Group was born. On March 31, 1958, the Prayer Group answered its first call of distress. That was the beginning of a miracle prayer ministry that has reached around the world. As word of this prayer ministry spread, calls increased until we now answer more than 20,000 telephone calls a month.

Intercessory prayer is a sacred calling and our Abundant Life Prayer Group realizes this. To meet the needs of the people is uppermost in their hearts and minds. They are ever prayerfully alert to impending tragedy when they answer a call. Just the other day the phone rang and as a prayer partner picked up the receiver to answer, a voice broke through with:

"I have a revolver loaded and ready to take my life . . . can you help me?"

The prayer partner spoke words of assurance to the would-be suicide and asked him to tell his story.

"For three days I have been locked in my room with my revolver loaded and ready to blow my brains out. But every time I start to pull the trigger I just chicken out . . . I'm just too miserable to live and too cowardly to die . . . what can I do . . .?" His voice trailed on in hopelessness as he said, "At one time I knew Jesus as my Savior, but I got away from Him. The farther I strayed from the Lord, the more my life became involved. I ended up serving a prison term. Now I have been released and have tried to go straight, but nobody wants to hire an ex-con. Life has lost its meaning and I just can't go on any longer — can you help me?"

His last question was drowned in convulsive sobs. The prayer partner compassionately told this man how Jesus is here in the now to give him a whole new life and how the power of God is still the same today, no matter how far he had strayed. After some time it was like the peace of God dawned inside the man. With this peace came the realization that God's miracle power was right there to restore life and health to him at the very point of his desperation. Soon the man was talking easily with the prayer partner in a way that was evident that he had found Christ as the answer to his need.

Finally, the prayer partner asked, "How did you happen to call the Abundant Life Prayer Group?"

"Not long ago a friend gave me this number and said, 'If you ever need help, call this number.'"

Of course, not all calls are suicidal but the requests do cover the gamut of human need. And each request is met with the same compassion and concern . . . and miracles happen.

At specific times I go to the Prayer Tower, sometimes to my own private room of prayer with the prayer requests from my friends and partners. Other times I go in to visit and pray with the Prayer Group. During these times they share with me some of the calls before we have prayer. The other night one prayer partner said, "I answered the phone with the usual, 'This is your Abundant Life Prayer Group.' Only uneasy breathing responded to my answer. Then the party hung up. In a few seconds, the phone light flashed again,

'May I help you, please?' This time, the same uneasy breathing and then violent sobs answered the question. Gradually gaining control of her voice, a young woman spoke:

" 'I thought once I wouldn't call, but I felt I just had to. I'm all mixed up and in a terrible mess. You just wouldn't understand if I told you.'

"I assured the young lady that I would try to understand if she wanted to relate her problem. Then in a trembling, tearful voice she said:

" 'I'm leaving my husband. I don't love him and I never did. I was forced to marry him and now we have a child. But I have stood it as long as I can; I'm leaving him today.'

"I assured her if she would put her trust in God that He would help her to find the answer to all her problems. Then we prayed together over the phone. The following day, the same young lady called. Now her voice was strong and confident as she said, 'I just wanted to thank you for your prayers. God has solved our problems and our home is reunited.' "

"We love our ministry," another prayer partner commented, "but prayer is hard work. We often become personally involved in the needs of the people who call. Like the mother, for instance, who called early one morning and said that the doctor had just called from the hospital to tell them their baby was dying. Later she called back to tell us that between the time they had called us and the time they reached the hospital, God answered prayer. The nurses met them in the hall with the good news that the baby had revived and was responding to treatment. Believe me, in a case like that, you get personally involved — you pray with compassion."

"Knowing how to listen is half the battle sometimes," another prayer partner said. "One night after I had listened to a man at length, he said, 'Thanks for listening and for just being there.'"

THE PRAYER TOWER ATTRACTS PEOPLE FROM ALL OVER THE WORLD

The Prayer Tower on the Oral Roberts University campus stands as a symbol of warmth, light, and hope. In more than 15 years of unwaivering, unbroken ministry, the Prayer Group has answered nearly two million calls from people all over the world — of all ages, in all walks of life, and with every conceivable problem under the sun.

Not only does the Prayer Group receive hundreds of calls and letters each day, but an equally astonishing number of visitors pour through the Prayer Tower on the ORU campus daily. Last summer a record number of 2,000 people visited the Prayer Tower in one day!

People came from as far as Africa, Australia, Brazil, Austria, Norway, Sweden, Israel, and all 50 states. Their professions were as varied and interesting as their comments — like the couple from Ohio. They walked in and the man was smiling from ear to ear. Finally, he said, "You know, we had to see this place. I felt I just had to tell you about my miracle." And this is what he said:

"One night I was at home when all of a sudden a pain struck my back and I couldn't move an inch. The pain was so intense that I couldn't stand the weight of my wife's hand upon my body. She started to call the doctor but decided to call the Abundant Life Prayer Group first. While she was still on the phone the Prayer Group prayed and my pain left immediately and I could again move freely. I am so thankful for the ministry of the Abundant Life Prayer

Group that we just had to come and see this wonderful place of prayer for ourselves."

Another man was from Russia. He had brought his father and his son to see the University and particularly the Prayer Tower. As he walked about the tower he just kept saying over and over, "God is real and miracles happen each day." Then he said, "God did for me as He did for Paul and Silas in the Philippian jail when He enabled me to escape from Russia." He of course could not divulge exactly how God delivered him but he gave all the credit to a miracle-working God. To him the Prayer Tower and the whole University were visible proof that God is still the God of miracles today.

This reminds me — recently a TV newscaster from Tulsa was in the Soviet Union where he purchased a copy of the Moscow News, an English edition published weekly by Izvestia Printshop. Much to his surprise he found a photograph and brief write-up on the Prayer Tower and ORU, which the Russian newspaper had reprinted from National Geographic magazine. So we thank God that the Prayer Tower is having an impact even in the areas of the world where prayer is not exactly in vogue. We have some dear wonderful Christian friends in Russia. Although they can't contact the Prayer Tower, the knowledge of its existence is a strength to their faith. We pray that one day they will have freedom to worship God as we do here in America.

Not all visitors come to the Prayer Tower to tell of miracles or to request prayer. Some, like the young man I mentioned earlier, are just simply intrigued with the architecture. For instance, an educator flew in from South Africa with his architect just to study the design of the Prayer Tower and other space-age facilities on the ORU campus. Then there was a special consultant from a university in

Jerusalem who came specifically to study the architectural structures on the campus. "It's an architect's mecca," one man was heard to exclaim.

In contrast was a little 83-year-old Seneca Indian lady, a descendant of a famous chief of the Seneca tribe. Although deeply religious in her own Indian faith, she has been a long-time follower and partner with me. She was deeply moved as she toured the Prayer Tower. She said, "What great faith it must have taken to build such a university."

Another couple who was especially intrigued with the Prayer Tower was Virginia and Ray, professional musicians who travel with a circus. They took their day off from the circus and came to visit the Prayer Tower and campus. When asked, "How did you know about Oral Roberts University?" Virginia answered:

"Who doesn't know about Oral Roberts? . . . we watch him all the time on television . . . " Then she added, "We've been all over this country and seen everything there is to see of any interest, but we've never seen anything like this . . . " Virginia, who has her Bachelor of Music degree, commented, "If I were young and starting all over again, I would come to ORU for my education . . . "

Then there are the vacationers — people like you and me — everyday people from all parts of the country and all walks of life. One such person, obviously weary and travel worn, said as she walked into the Prayer Tower, "I can hardly believe I am really here . . . "

Tears filled her eyes as she said, "But after being here and absorbing this atmosphere, I'm not tired anymore — I feel so lifted up . . . " Comments similar to this are heard often in the Prayer Tower. There is a serenity in the very atmosphere here that lifts you and gives you a shot of new life that can come only from God.

There is really no way I could relate to you all the miracles that have happened in answer to prayer when people call the Prayer Tower. We hear of new miracles every day. I just know that the Prayer Tower and the Prayer Group continues to be many things to many people. To me, personally, it is like a shield around me. I know they call my name in prayer many times a day. I feel this in my spirit. The lights never go out in the Prayer Tower. The Abundant Life Prayer Group is on duty 24 hours a day, 365 days a year. Every 8 hours, a group changes. Sometimes, it seems that the longest, loneliest hours are from midnight 'til dawn. But our prayer partners don't mind because they know that the morning will dawn a better day for the hundreds of people who will dial:

918 • 743-7971

Tulsa, Oklahoma

and hear a reassuring voice across the miles, say:

"Abundant Life Prayer Group . . . May I help you?" My Friend, I want you to know that you have my personal invitation to call the Prayer Tower any time — day or night — when you or a loved one is in distress. You can experience miracles in your life just as the thousands of others who call each month. Remember:

GOD MADE MIRACLES FOR YOU AND YOU FOR MIRACLES.